Cambridge Elements ☰

Elements in Music since 1945
edited by
Mervyn Cooke
University of Nottingham

MUSIC TRANSFORMING CONFLICT

Ariana Phillips-Hutton
University of Cambridge

CAMBRIDGE
UNIVERSITY PRESS

CAMBRIDGE
UNIVERSITY PRESS

University Printing House, Cambridge CB2 8BS, United Kingdom

One Liberty Plaza, 20th Floor, New York, NY 10006, USA

477 Williamstown Road, Port Melbourne, VIC 3207, Australia

314–321, 3rd Floor, Plot 3, Splendor Forum, Jasola District Centre,
New Delhi – 110025, India

79 Anson Road, #06–04/06, Singapore 079906

Cambridge University Press is part of the University of Cambridge.

It furthers the University's mission by disseminating knowledge in the pursuit of
education, learning, and research at the highest international levels of excellence.

www.cambridge.org
Information on this title: www.cambridge.org/9781108813105
DOI: 10.1017/9781108891363

First published 2020

A catalogue record for this publication is available from the British Library.

ISBN 978-1-108-81310-5 Paperback
ISSN 2632-7783 (print)
ISSN 2632-7791 (online)

Music Transforming Conflict

Elements in Music since 1945

DOI : 10.1017/9781108891363
First published online: October 2020

Ariana Phillips-Hutton
University of Cambridge

Author for correspondence: Ariana Phillips-Hutton, asp38@cam.ac.uk

Abstract : Teach the world to sing, and all will be in perfect harmony – or so the songs tell us. Music is widely believed to unify and bring peace, but the focus on music as a vehicle for fostering empathy and reconciliation between opposing groups threatens to overly simplify our narratives of how interpersonal conflict might be transformed. In this Element, I offer a critique of empathy's ethical imperative of radical openness and position the acknowledgement of moral responsibility as a fundamental component of music's capacity to transform conflict. Through case studies of music and conflict transformation in Australia and Canada, I assess the complementary roles of musically mediated empathy and guilt in post-conflict societies and argue that a consideration of musical and moral implication as part of studies on music and conflict offers a powerful tool for understanding music's potential to contribute to societal change.

Keywords : guilt, empathy, conflict transformation, Secret Path, Sorry Song

ISBNs : 9781108813105 (PB), 9781108891363 (OC)
ISSNs : 2632–7783 (print), 2632–7791 (online)

Contents

1 How Can Music Help?

The preface to Gary Ansdell's book *How Music Helps in Music Therapy and in Everyday Life* contains a series of salutary warnings against readerly disappointment in the implementation of the title's promise. Music, we discover, does not always help, nor should we consider it a mere instrument for personal or societal repair (Ansdell, 2014, xvi–xviii). It has the power to contribute to human flourishing that may be therapeutic in application, but is not a panacea. Though this Element examines music's potential to help in a rather different context, a similar 'dear reader' moment seems to be appropriate here. And so, I offer my own caveats.

First, in what follows I explore both the descriptive ('in what ways') and explanatory ('by what means') aspects implicit in the question of 'how' music may be transformative of conflict. This traverses several distinct areas of study, from peacebuilding and philosophy to the political and cognitive sciences to several distinct strands of music studies. These explorations are not exhaustive. This is partly due to the concise nature of this format and partly due to a desire to open up a broader field of enquiry for studying music and conflict.

Second, both 'music' and 'conflict' are terms that encompass a range of situations and practices. In the next section, 'Theorising Conflict Transformation', I offer a definition of conflict as centred around negative relations, but I have deliberately left music under-defined. While the case studies focus on specific pieces and performances from broadly Western traditions, I write of music in general as a set of sonic relations negotiated and enacted in real-time performance and configured according to local conventions. In some traditions, including Western art music, these relations are partially determined by music as an object (e.g. a score), while regulating factors in other musical forms might be recordings, performance styles, or oral traditions. Even though the connections between sound and body, or between score, recording, and performance vary according to cultural-historical context, they constitute music, nonetheless. Music is multiple: at once activities, objects, and ideas about what those activities and objects are, do, and mean for particular people at a particular time.

Third, music in its multiplicity has many uses and effects. To argue for 'music transforming conflict' is not to suggest a further instrumentalisation of an abstract entity but an effort to come to grips with another facet of how people (as individuals and as groups) experience music and music-making in the world. Like all such efforts, this entails simplification and generalisation.

Finally, conflict transformation in any form is itself radically dependent on the commitment of individuals and societies to its difficult work. There is no magic pill, musical or otherwise, and the sobering assessment by Charles

Villa-Vicencio, former Director of the South African Truth and Reconciliation Commission, remains as relevant now as it was when it was penned twenty years ago: 'To expect every South African to undergo a cathartic experience in dealing with the past is to expect everyone to be caught up in the enthusiasm of an evangelical preacher on a Sunday morning. In reality, most people do not even show up to hear the sermon' (1999, 199).

Although this Element may contain elements of preaching to the converted, it is not an evangelical tract for music's usefulness within conflict transformation; rather, it takes a close look at the reasons scholars give for believing music can be transformative in order to determine whether those assessments of its potential are accurate. Following this introduction, the remainder of the first section 'How Can Music Help?' falls into two subsections, first introducing theories of conflict and its transformation before examining prevalent roles for music in conflict transformation. The next section, 'Constructing Transformation' expands on several themes that run throughout the remainder of the argument, from the complementary roles of musically mediated empathy and guilt to the impact of participatory and presentational performance formats on musical conflict transformation. In the ensuing sections, 'Singing Sorry' and 'Chanie's Story', I present two case studies in musical conflict transformation before offering, in conclusion, some comparative assessment ('Reckoning with Sonic Histories') and suggestions for future approaches to music, conflict, and guilt ('How Music Can Help').

In many respects, this Element is the product of what the political theorist Hannah Arendt (1958) and others call the *vita contemplativa*, an abstract sphere of life characterised by reason, knowledge, and thinking that complements the *vita activa* of labour, work, and action. In it, I bring together and build upon work in a number of fields that touch on questions of music and conflict, particularly that of applied ethnomusicology. This juxtapositional style of thinking allows me to map out unexpected relationships and to ask how musical practices speak to and alongside one another. In examining how thinking shapes actions (and conversely, how actions shape thought) I expose the vital tension between philosophical contemplation and the ways in which human relationships are manifested, negotiated, and transformed in and through music.

In short, I ask two questions: first, what is it possible to say about the relationship between music and conflict transformation? Second, how might we (as scholars, as musicians, as human beings in a conflict-ridden world) think about it more deeply? These questions stem from a conviction that understanding how music makes conflict transformation available in new ways opens up possibilities for a fuller understanding of human experience. The prevalence of open and barely concealed conflicts in contemporary society over racial injustice, economic deprivation, religious identity, political disenfranchisement, ecological collapse – not to mention the number of musicians and organisations working to transform these and other conflicts – suggests that the answers to these questions are a matter of particular urgency in music since 1945.

* * *

In 1972, the anthropologist Gregory Bateson posited that the arts are a special form of communication that has primarily to do with psychic integration and identity (Bateson, 1972, esp. 128–52). This integration might apply to the social bonding amongst members of the same group, but it might apply equally (and perhaps even more forcefully) to the integration of different parts of the individual self, and of individual and group selves with the world at large. In all of these contexts, the arts allow for individuals and groups to articulate and enact their various identities in the world. More recently, the ethnomusicologist Thomas Turino (2008, 18) paired this integrative function with an imaginative one when he suggested that 'artistic processes crystallize the very essence of a good life by dramatically emphasizing the interplay of future possibilities with experiences and things we already know from the past – all within [...] a specially framed and engrossing present'. The capacity of art to model ways of being through promoting identity formation and expression lies at the heart of anthropological arguments for its centrality to human evolution and survival. Fittingly, this also underlies many of the arguments suggesting that the arts have the potential to effect positive social change, whether by increasing individual wellbeing and improving health outcomes or by repairing fractured community ties and facilitating mutual understanding between different groups. This is a common feature of arts-based research as a whole, but in spite of (or perhaps due to) its non-representational character, often music is accorded a privileged position among the arts when it comes to this integrative and imaginative function.

Outside the context of academic scholarship, belief in music's particular power to unify disparate groups and heal interpersonal conflict is commonplace, assumed by everything from Hollywood movies (think of the boombox seren-ade in 1989's *Say Anything . . .* or Heath Ledger's rendition of 'Can't Take My Eyes Off of You' in 1999's *10 Things I Hate About You*) to advertisements (e.g. Vertigo Music's 'Share Music. Share Life.' campaign), to arts initiative funding committees and non-governmental organisations (NGOs) working in societies riven by current or past conflict. In the context of romantic comedies or marketing campaigns, the assumption that the appropriate grand gesture accom-plished through music offers a conduit to restoring positive relationships is perhaps naïve, but is otherwise relatively trivial. However, in the case of interpersonal conflict on a larger scale, the role of music becomes more complicated and a failure to interrogate it more consequential. Within the broad disciplines of peace studies and conflict transformation, this has resulted in a raft of initiatives and academic studies that focus on the arts in general – and on music in particular – as a means of mitigating the damaging psychosocial aspects of violent conflict, or what Arild Bergh and John Sloboda (2010, 4) term the 'traumas and other invisible effects of war'. This attentiveness to music as mitigation has found particular expression within music studies in the sub-discipline of applied ethnomusicology, which is 'guided by principles of social responsibility' and seeks to put ethnomusicological knowledge to use 'toward solving concrete problems' in society (ICTM, 2007; for more, see Harrison, Mackinlay, and Pettan, 2010; Pettan and Titon, 2015). Yet despite this surge of scrutiny, the foundations for this conflict-transforming capacity of the arts remain only partially understood.

Thinking more deeply about the roles musical activities play in long-term processes of conflict transformation has the potential to open up new perspectives on both music and conflict. In particular, this Element confronts the normative underpinnings of current approaches to music and conflict transformation by critiquing their often-implicit reliance on an ethically inflected discourse of empathy. While empathy may play a significant role, I position it alongside the acknowledgement of guilt and moral responsibility as a fundamental component of music's potential to transform conflict: through interlinking processes of identification and symbolisation enacted in music-making, participants are confronted with narratives of guilt and encouraged to accept their implication in the experiences of others. After marking out the theoretical ground, I then present two short case studies in music and conflict transformation in order to demonstrate how composers, performers, and audiences are already producing musical narratives of conflict that include, at least implicitly, the acknowledgement of moral responsibility as part of the reconciliatory process. This Element is thus structured first as an argument for expanding the discussion around music and conflict transformation, and then an exemplification through music case studies of how including themes of guilt, implication, and moral responsibility can shift the interpretation and understanding of how and to what extent music can help.

1.1 Theorising Conflict Transformation

A basic problem in thinking about the relationship between the arts and conflict transformation stems from the need to differentiate types of conflict and transformative responses to them. Just as individual relationships differ from those between societal groups or between nations, so too do the requirements for dealing with conflict in each. Even within a particular relationship 'category', what conflict and its transformation look (or sound) like will vary both geographically and culturally, and is likely to change over time. In order to make sense of the role of the arts – in this case, music – in transforming conflict, we need to begin with a clear understanding of both conflict itself and approaches to its transformation.

Our sketch of the contours of conflict begins by acknowledging that it is a manifold phenomenon that can occur on one or more personal, relational, structural, or cultural levels; conflict is a negative relation existing in different shades and intensities that characterises the continuum between 'war' and 'peace'.[1] In this sense, conflict implies the possibility of its own dissolution in a state of idealised concord. Its frequently episodic character (whether the eruption of an interpersonal argument or the outbreak of war) encourages the perception of it as a discrete situation arising within a particular time frame; however, pioneering peace studies scholar John Paul Lederach argues that conflicts also possess an epicentre, or a 'web of relational patterns, often providing a history of lived episodes, from which new episodes and issues emerge' (2003, 31). The intersection of immediate causes and underlying patterns of relationship (many of which touch on questions of identity, individualism, and authority) make untangling the origins of specific conflicts especially challenging.

The complex structure of conflict is mirrored in the multivalence of conflict transformation, which is at once a way of comprehending the phenomenon of conflict and a collection of practices aimed at mitigating its effects. Understood as an analytical framework, conflict transformation 'seeks to understand social conflict as it emerges from and produces change in [...] human experience' (Lederach, 2003, 26), while as a strategy of intervention it applies this understanding to promote 'constructive processes' that effect change. As an intervention, transforming conflict requires addressing both the immediate content of a particular conflictual moment, and its wider context. In the short term, the specific forms of redress are often ephemeral and context-specific, designed to provide solutions to immediate problems; over time, however, they generate adaptive responses that can transform structural aspects of conflict through increasing justice, reducing violence, and restoring or reconfiguring personal relationships.

Thus far, I have referenced the use of the arts as a tool for *transforming* conflict, but within the broad area of peace and conflict studies, the rhetoric of

---

[1] Of course, neither war nor peace is a static state. All of these are dynamic and constantly evolving.

transformation is itself controversial. Other potential terms include conflict settlement, management, and resolution, each of which indicates competing orientations towards conflict. The phrase 'conflict transformation' dates from the 1980s and is associated with Lederach (2003, esp. 3–5). Lederach argues that focusing on the settlement or resolution of conflict tends to avoid addressing the fundamental relational issues that cause conflict in favour of prioritising premature agreement, conciliation, and outside arbitration. Transformation, on the other hand, pursues a dual-sided process: the cessation of an undesirable situation accompanied by the construction of a more desirable one. It is thus primarily concerned with the transitional stage between conflict and post-conflict known as peacebuilding (as opposed to peacekeeping or peacemaking).[2]

In rebuttal, proponents of 'resolution', including Oliver Ramsbotham, Tom Woodhouse, and Hugh Miall, claim that transformation is what is going on at the deepest level of conflict resolution, and note that – despite its positive connotations – transformation is a fundamentally indeterminate term of change that doesn't specify how, or in what direction, a conflict may be transformed (2011, 9–10). While the objections they raise are persuasive, it seems to me that conflict resolution nonetheless emphasises the ending of something undesirable – and therefore reveals an orientation towards definitive or final fixes. Speaking of conflict settlement takes this static future orientation a step further with its connotations of finality and stability, while conflict management suggests a distinctly top-down approach that sidelines social change in favour of social control. In contrast, transformation suggests a process of ongoing change in the causes of conflict with the ultimate goal of constructing new social relations. In the context of music and conflict, thinking about the potential for transformation focuses attention on the processual, temporal character of music; moreover, transformation's heightened rhetoric is congruent with the discourse that accompanies many musical efforts at confronting the causes and contexts of conflict.

Closely related to this debate over transformation is the presumed aim of reconciliation at the close of conflict. Etymologically speaking, to reconcile derives from Anglo-Norman (*reconciler*) and Latin (*reconciliāre*) and means to re-establish, restore, or to win back, usually in the context of restoring friendly relations between people or between an individual and God/the Christian church.[3] In modern-day peacebuilding practice, there are multiple explanations of what reconciliation might look like – alongside some disagreement over

---

[2] For more on this three-part model see Sandole (1998).
[3] *Oxford English Dictionary*, 3rd ed. (2009), s.v. 'reconcile, v.'.

whether it should be the end goal of conflict transformation at all.[4] Opponents argue that reconciliation is too enmeshed in a vision of communitarian social philosophy (based on the work of John Rawls and Jürgen Habermas) that may have limited meaning in situations where previous social relations between groups were violent or discriminatory. When social groups do not have a positive history of relationship, bringing them back together risks restoring the social patterns that contributed to the conflict in the first place: for groups with no history of conciliation, what is there to reconcile? Supporters of reconciliation, such as the sociologist Johan Galtung, insist that true reconciliation is not the turning back of the societal clock but a deeper work of restoration: 'the process of healing the traumas of both victims and perpetrators after violence, providing a closure of the bad relation' (Galtung, 2001, 3–4). While it is not my purpose here to evaluate the specific form reconciliation might take in a particular conflict, Galtung's description of reconciliation as a newly negotiated relationship provides a welcome foundation for increasing attentiveness to the change and flux of reconciliatory processes.

The increasing interest in conflict transformation and reconciliation – especially on the level of the nation state – is itself evidence of a shift in the perception of accountability for conflict and the necessity of taking concrete action to mitigate its effects. Throughout history, governments have perpetuated horrific violence on the people and lands under their control, but the idea that they, or their successors, might be held to account by a court of law, officially apologise, or make restitution for their actions is a relatively new one.[5] Accordingly, there are multiple models for how societies have pursued reconciliation in the wake of serious violent conflict. Often, this has involved criminal proceedings against perpetrators of violence, and with this development has come a raft of new terminology. For example, the first charge of committing 'crimes [...] against humanity' is the 1915 statement by the governments of Great Britain, France, and Russia declaring the Ottoman government responsible for the massacres of ethnic Armenian civilians taking place in what is now Turkey, and the first prosecutions to use this rubric occurred in 1945–6 at the International Military Tribunal in Nuremberg.[6] Many organisations now describe

---

[4] See, for example, essays by Sonali Chakravorty, Erix Doxtader, and Adrian Little in Hirsch (2012).

[5] The mistreatment of people has a lengthy and ongoing use as a pretext for military conflict and current efforts at providing legal remedies often are imperfectly applied (witness the recent case brought in the International Court of Justice by The Gambia against Myanmar over its treatment of the Rohingya people).

[6] The history of the phrase 'crimes against humanity' extends back well into the nineteenth century, where it was applied first to the slave trade, and later as a description of the Belgian government's actions in the Congo. The phrase 'laws of humanity' also appears in the Martens clause of the Hague Conventions of 1899 and 1907, but the Hague Conventions specifically apply only to

the Ottoman Empire's extermination of ethnic Armenians as 'genocide', and this term, coined by Raphael Lemkin in 1943, has been applied retrospectively to a number of other events. Genocide was not prosecuted as a specific crime until 1993's International Criminal Tribunal for the Former Yugoslavia. Across the intervening years, the high-profile spectacle of political and military leaders being tried (or escaping trial) for various violent acts has focused attention on the legal processes of establishing criminal guilt and retributive justice.

Despite the prominence of legal remediation in the past century, not all societies that have suffered conflicts have chosen to address it through establishing and punishing guilty parties. Cultural theorist Paul Connerton (2012) notes that obligatory forgetting imposed by the state has a long history, beginning at least as early as 403 BC with an Athenian proclamation forbidding the remembrance of crimes committed during a period of civil strife. Another historical example of prescriptive forgetting as part of a peace process is the Treaty of Westphalia (1648), which enjoined all sides to forget the horrific violence of the Thirty Years' War, while more subtle forms occurred in post-World War II West Germany, Austria, and France, where retributive processes of de-Nazification were suppressed by the 1950s for the sake of establishing cohesion in civil society. These examples are joined by one of the best-known acts of state-imposed amnesia in the twentieth century, which occurred after the death of the Spanish dictator Francisco Franco in 1975. Spain's Pact of Forgetting and Amnesty Law helped solidify the transition to democratic rule, but at the (still-controversial) cost of neglecting opportunities to establish what happened both under the oppressions of Franco's rule, and in the Spanish Civil War that preceded it. These examples demonstrate the social desire for stability and a sense of moving forward that also underpins David Rieff's critique *In Praise of Forgetting* (2016), which argues that continuous remembering of past traumas damages both the public and the state by excoriating wounds that should be left alone to heal.

Yet perhaps neither meting out justice nor adopting a policy of forgetting holds the key to transforming conflict. One increasingly common model, and the most important one for my purposes, is that which goes under the name of transitional justice. This is a comparatively young field encompassing the 'full range of processes and mechanisms associated with a society's attempt to come

---

conditions of war between states and therefore do not cover actions taken by a government against its own civilians. See Clark (2011). According to the Rome Statute of the International Criminal Court, genocidal acts are those 'committed with intent to destroy, in whole or in part, a national, ethnic, racial or religious group', whilst crimes against humanity are acts 'committed as part of a widespread or systematic attack directed against any civilian population', https://bit.ly/3hbaxol (accessed 7 January 2020).

to terms with a legacy of large-scale past abuses, in order to ensure accountability, serve justice and achieve reconciliation' (United Nations, 2010, 2). As such, it is closely aligned with a therapeutic vision of reconciliation and with many tenets of conflict transformation. Transitional justice often emphasises the role of truth; some of the most visible mechanisms of transitional justice are truth-seeking initiatives such as the 'truth commission', an official, but non-judicial, inquiry that investigates patterns of past abuses. More than forty of these have been established around the world since the 1970s.[7] The purpose of such non-judicial commissions varies by location, but a common model, exemplified by Peru's Truth and Reconciliation Commission (2001–3) and Timor-Leste's Commission for Reception, Truth and Reconciliation (2002–5), attempts to bring out the truth about human rights violations undertaken by repressive states or by non-state actors as a means of encouraging reconciliation between various ethnic, religious, or social groups. In such cases, truth encompasses both *knowledge*, configured here as the recovery of factual histories of the past, and *acknowledgement*, by which I mean the sanctioning of this knowledge, or the making it a 'part of the public cognitive scene' (Thomas Nagel, qtd. in Weschler 1989, 93).

In theory, these approaches to conflict transformation and reconciliation apply equally to minor interpersonal conflicts and to entrenched intergroup or systemic violence, but in practice there is relatively little crossover between those areas in either the broad fields of study that touch on conflict or in the subfield of music and conflict transformation. On a small scale, interpersonal conflict is more often the province of, on the one hand, psychology, and on the other, music therapy and community music studies (see Stige et al., 2010). Meanwhile, within peace/conflict studies, substantial amounts of scholarly work on large-scale conflict transformation has focused on 'headline' situations in places that have suffered recent or ongoing violent conflict such as Colombia, Guatemala, South Africa, Rwanda, the Balkans, and Israel/Palestine; the same geopolitical areas have featured prominently in examinations of the relationship between music and conflict transformation (from an extensive literature, see Gray, 2008; Pinto García, 2014; Pruitt, 2011; Sugarman, 2010; Zelizer, 2003).

Although the case studies that appear in 'Singing Sorry' and 'Chanie's Story' later in this Element exhibit similarities to other work done in studies of music and conflict, certain distinctions are evident. For example, they both focus on musical engagement with the histories of white settler colonialism and its integral violence against Indigenous populations, rather than on recent armed

---

[7] See the reports provided by *Amnesty International*, www.amnesty.org/download/Documents/40000/pol300042010en.pdf and by the *United States Institute of Peace*, https://bit.ly/2YebR2t (accessed 7 January 2020).

conflicts. These are conflicts that have been characterised by one-sided violence couched in (and cloaked by) legal language and government policies which served to distance their impact from wider society, but they are also conflicts which have recently come to national attention in new ways after decades of activism. The musical examples I have chosen are presented in 'local' (here Western-influenced) musical styles and are anchored in specific communities and the stories of individuals in Australia and Canada, respectively, but they also envision societal transformation on a grand scale. Composers, performers, and other associated individuals and institutions have integrated them into transitional justice efforts (including within education) as catalysts for a widespread reckoning with the past. The configurations of musical conflict transformation they demonstrate exemplify the particular role played by music as a sounded-in-time relation in both the recovery and broadcasting of factual truth and the conversion of those facts into knowledge sanctioned by institutions and by society at large. In this sense, then, the case studies will show how music helps in establishing truth about conflicts and, thus, in promoting reconciliation as part of long-term change processes of conflict transformation.

1.2 Studying Music and Conflict

The belief that music-making and listening can influence social behaviour, often coupled with assertions about the differing effects of musical types, runs deep in a wide variety of philosophical traditions.[8] From this, one might expect the types of music used in conflict transformation to follow a discernible pattern, but beyond a general eschewal of specific genres or pieces that might contribute to conflict through inflammatory elements, musical activities used in conflict transformation exhibit astounding variety. Given its high prestige, it is perhaps unsurprising that Western art music is a frequent option: classical music education programmes such as Venezuela's *El Sistema* have been widely popular as models for conflict transformation. In neighbouring Colombia, the state-funded *Música para la reconciliación* uses choral and instrumental ensembles to develop what the organisation terms musical, civic, and cognitive competencies among populations impacted by the nearly forty-year-long armed conflict in the country. Their website highlights the story of a young man named Miguel Antonio who aspires to study double bass at university and leads music classes for children; yet, underneath tracking shots of him clutching his instrument on the back of a motorcycle is not a snippet of art music, but the driving rhythms of

---

[8] Plato (*The Republic*) and Aristotle (*Politics*) are the best-known advocates in the Western philosophical tradition, but see also the writings of Confucius (*Yue Ji*). More recent thinkers who have taken up such a position include Roger Scruton (2014) and Peter Kivy (2009a, 2009b).

Colombia's national dance, *cumbia*.[9] This conjunction of traditions highlights the recent focus on popular genres and especially on song in conflict transformation efforts. The incorporation of popular traditions is often a sign of a more grassroots approach: for example, María Elisa Pinto García (2014) traces how Colombian performers operating outside of official reconciliation efforts compose raps and *vallenato* songs to tell of their experiences of displacement and violence. While not all genres have the same potential for conflict transformation (Pinto García highlights the limitations of the harsh lyrics used by Colombian rappers), those that exhibit a high level of collaboration or allow for significant personal agency in narrating a story are particularly widespread.

In addition to diversity in genre, music plays various roles in transforming societies suffering from recent conflict; these include official or semi-official events such as concerts or CD releases organised in the name of peace for conflict-torn countries (Seeds of Peace, 2006), the symbolic return of music or of key performers to contested or destroyed locations (Beckles Willson, 2009; Sprigge, 2019), and the renovation or creation of new institutions for musical study and performance (Haskell, 2015). This is conflict transformation in the sense of changing the everyday material conditions under which music is made and experienced. On a more individual or therapeutic scale are community efforts centred on personal healing and the preservation of cultural heritage, including the use of songwriting and performance by victims of violence (Pinto García, 2014; Ritter, 2014), the creation of community music groups (Robertson, 2008; Softic, 2011; Zelizer, 2003), and the integration of refugees into their host society through multicultural musical learning (Skyllstad, 1995, 2000, 2008). Here, music is a tool for transforming perceptions of history, of community, and of the 'others' in society. At times these musical activities intersect with larger sociopolitical projects of conflict transformation, such as in South Africa's transition to majority rule in the 1990s, where every session of their Truth and Reconciliation Commission included the communal singing of hymns along with the national anthem (newly stitched together out of the apartheid-era anthem 'Die Stem van Suid-Afrika' and the isiXhosa hymn 'Nkosi Sikelel' iAfrika'), or in post-1994 Rwanda, where an entire subgenre of genocide commemoration songs has elevated some artists to household names.

Despite the fact that a disproportionate amount of research has examined musical activity as a means of ameliorating conflict, music educator Felicity

---

[9] Fundación Batuta, 'La música como herramienta de paz en Quibdó', www.fundacionbatuta.org/reconciliacion.php (accessed 7 January 2020). Like *El Sistema*, *Música para la reconciliación* is interested in social transformation (here, counteracting poverty and deprivation) in addition to conflict transformation; for more on the difficulties such projects face, see Geoffrey Baker's (2018) damning indictment of *El Sistema*.

Laurence (2008, 33) notes that imparting peace remains one of music's least common uses. Increasing recognition of this interpretive doubleness means that music's 'dark side' in exacerbating conflict has also received substantial attention in recent years, from the use of music as an instrument of torture to music that legitimises violence (Cusick, 2006; Pilzer, 2014; see also Grant et al., 2010 for an overview). Here, the 1994 genocide in Rwanda provides one of the most prominent examples of the complexities of studying music as potential accessory to conflict: the case of the well-known musician Simon Bikindi, who was charged with fomenting genocide ideology by the International Criminal Tribunal of Rwanda. As legal scholar James Parker (2015, 2) makes clear, the spectacle of 'a major international legal institution alleging a *singer* to have been among the ninety-three "most responsible"' for the killing of at least half a million people in 1994 should make anyone with an interest in music's role in society take notice. Throughout Bikindi's trial, song served as evidence or object (though its sonic components were routinely ignored) and as mode of address (both Bikindi and other witnesses sang to and for the court, as well as, in Bikindi's case, beyond the court to the listening public). Bikindi himself was figured alternately as 'a Siren or Orpheus', and his music as overwhelmingly powerful, capable of enticing others towards either harmless cultural celebration or genocide (see Parker, 2015, 63–84). Though Bikindi was convicted on a different (non-musical) charge in 2010, the potency of music as both a check and impetus to conflict was highlighted in 2014 with the arrest and imprisonment of popular gospel singer and Rwandan genocide survivor Kizito Mihigo, believed by many to be in part due to his song lyrics criticising the official narrative of the genocide (Rosen, 2014; see McCoy, 2009 for more on music and the Rwandan genocide). What Bruce Johnson and Martin Cloonan (2008, 1) call music's 'radical ambiguity' in relationship with conflict suggests once more that music's capacity to intervene in a positive fashion must be carefully assessed.

The global scope of this wealth of research on music and conflict is impressive, and considering the kinds of musical and social relations these case studies reflect and produce is a key component in answering more abstract questions about music-making and conflict. Yet under close examination, some lacunae appear. Much of the research within the various branches of musicology and anthropology has been presented as ethnographic case studies, which provide a deep understanding of particular moments within conflict transformation, but at the same time render meaningful comparative analysis difficult. Likewise, music-based interventions by NGOs and similar organisations can capture the texture of particular conflicts, but may shed little light on broader trends. This has also limited examination of the reasons for music's impact in different contexts. For example, empirical data on the impact of short- and long-term musical interventions or different aims and types of musical activities is a feature of many studies, but synthesising information about multiple locations or kinds of conflict is not. While cross-cultural comparisons must be carefully calibrated, juxtaposing examples of primary and secondary ethnographic analysis to highlight different aspects has the potential to suggest broad patterns within music and conflict transformation and thereby contribute to creating flexible conceptual frameworks that guide what the ethnomusicologist Marcia Herndon (borrowing from data science and bioinformatics) calls 'tertiary analysis' (2000, 351), or the interpretation of data within a general context.

In particular, the ethnographic focus of research on music and conflict within applied ethnomusicology has meant that theorising why music should foster reconciliation has often played only a minor role (partial exceptions include Araujó, 2006; Dieckmann and Davidson, 2019); however, in related fields, a number of reasons have been put forth to explain why music might be uniquely powerful in processes of unification and healing – and therefore well-suited to conflict transformation. Researchers in psychology and phenomenology have noted music's power to initiate processes of entrainment (Jones and Boltz, 1989), to encourage prosocial behaviour (Greitemeyer, 2009), and to regulate emotions (Saarikallio, 2010). Others have focused on more general characteristics of music: these include its ubiquity in modern life, its emotive character, and what Ian Cross (1999) has described as its 'floating intentionality', or its sense of an indeterminate meaningfulness that allows individuals to project different determinate meanings onto it. Music sociologist Tia DeNora focuses on music's capacity to shape our sense of self, considering music as a 'technology of the self' or 'a cultural resource that actors may mobilize for their on-going work of self-construction' (1999, 32), while Joel Krueger (2019) draws on the '4E' approach to cognitive science in suggesting that music's capacity to 'scaffold' new kinds of thought and experience is linked to its material and worldmaking character. In these approaches, music figures as a ubiquitous connection between an outer social world and an inner psychological one, but perhaps most importantly, the activity of performing, listening to, or participating in music (what Christopher Small [1998] calls 'musicking') is seen as offering a perspective on what it is like to be a human that is at once 'rich, diverse, and globally distributed' (Clarke, 2019, 63). Considering these facets together suggests that musical participation can expose us to new ways of being in the world that are at once cognitive, embodied, and affective. This participation in music becomes, to borrow Simon Frith's (1996, 275) description, 'a fusion of imaginative fantasy and bodily practice' that is simultaneously an 'integration of aesthetics and ethics' – and one that has the potential to act powerfully in our world.

The twin focus on the embodied experience of music and on significant encounters through musical activity links much of this scholarly research within a non-representational paradigm that approaches music studies as inclusive of meaningful experiences outside the traditional domains of rhetoric and semiotics. On the one hand, this is related to the broader 'affective turn' in the humanities that prioritises theorising about 'how bodies and bodily matter participate in the ongoing construction of the social and, ultimately, politics and the political' (Stirling, 2018, 54; see also Clough, 2007; Gregg and Siegworth, 2010). On the other hand, it is related to the growing prominence of practice-based research conducted by scholars, practitioners, and activists interested in exploring the concrete effects of particular musical interventions in social life. Linking the abstract and the concrete remains a distinct challenge in many fields of music studies, but music and conflict provides a particularly productive domain in which to examine the interactions of these multiple spheres.

One of the most productive areas of research on the potential power of music to effect reconciliation or conflict transformation has focused on music's capacity for providing points of attachment or identification between groups, what Charles Keil memorably referred to as the 'urge to merge' (Keil and Feld, 1984, 98). Something of music's force in effecting this cohesion is brought out in the parallels between an audience's participation (in the broad sense) in music and in a sport such as football. For example, both activities involve joint attention, communal participation, and interaction with others. The experience of watching a football game or listening to a performance together with others can generate positive community feeling by connecting individuals and identity groups through shared affect – often accompanied or indeed cemented by coordinated physical action (swaying, clapping, cheering, etc.). In comparison to sport, music possesses the additional advantage of involving everyone all the time; it is less oppositional in character and more accommodating of different skill levels and modes of participation. Moreover, because music gives primacy to sound, it can operate across space in ways that generate social solidarity even when physical proximity is limited (a feature that is especially notable as social isolation is enforced in many places around the world as I write in 2020).[10] These characteristics make it unsurprising that sport and music are two of most

---

[10] The relationship between sound, vision, proximity, and feelings of sociality (or lack thereof) cuts in multiple directions and has a growing literature in sound studies; I can barely scratch the surface here, but from a historical perspective, see Alejandra Bronfman (2016) and Frantz Fanon (1965) on the development of the radio in the Caribbean and Algeria, respectively; see also Peter McMurray (2019) for a thought-provoking study of mediated witnessing in relation to contemporary audiovisual documentation of police brutality.

common activities supported by NGOs and other organisations working to transform conflict.

Yet investigating any capacity to bring people together – to generate feelings of unity – must be balanced by the acknowledgement that music's meanings are open and malleable. Musical meanings are multivalent: constantly negotiated by people engaging with music and with the sonic spaces and interpersonal networks that music affords. This is why, in his introduction to the edited collection *Music and Conflict*, John M. O'Connell suggests that it is music's interpretive flexibility that gives it a particular advantage in addressing conflict:

> Music rather than language may provide a better medium for interrogating the character of conflict and for evaluating the quality of conflict resolution. While language as prose tends to delimit interpretation according to the partial dictates of authorial intention, music as practice serves to liberate interpretation according to the multiple views of audience reception. (O'Connell, 2010, 2)

In other words, music's susceptibility to different interpretations can allow participants the intellectual space necessary for finding a shared togetherness or reality in the midst of conflict. The metaphor of music as providing emotional and intellectual breathing space resonates with Arild Bergh's (2011) suggestion that participating in music can be a beneficial diversion that interrupts fraught moments, thereby increasing the potential for further breakthroughs. Moreover, music can mediate these experiences in ways that are widely accessible, yet may be perceived as less purposeful and consequential than those of language, which gives it a particular force in managing situations of social and individual uncertainty (Cross, 2012, esp. 319–20). Positioning music as an opportunity to increase felt affective intensity while decreasing defensive affective responses to a perceived threat seems like a paradox, but it is one that hinges on music's ability to provide for moments of seeming similarity amongst participants.

At times, musically mediated similarities may be elusive or directed in ways that are undesirable; as such, scholars, musicians, and institutions must remain alert to the fact that increasing group identification through music is as likely to reinforce existing social boundaries as to break them down.[11] This doubleness at the heart of music's capacity for group-formation also points to one of the fundamental incongruences facing the academic study of music and conflict transformation: the persistent belief in music's power counterpoised with the difficulty in assessing concretely its capacity for motivating change. Paired with

---

[11] There is another parallel to the use, for example, of football chants as identity markers. For more on music's reinforcement of social boundaries see also McCann (1995).

developments in the psychology of music, a genuine desire among many scholars to provide evidence for music's social usefulness, and the vestiges of romantic rhetoric about the powers of music, there are occasional moments of over-optimism. Thus, Olivier Urbain rhapsodises about music as possessing 'a tremendous power to move people in any direction, towards peaceful and noble goals, or violent and destructive ones' (Urbain, 2008, 1), while in the same volume Anne-Marie Gray characterises music as a 'bridge between a shared past and reconciliation. It allows a society to understand itself in terms of its own interpretation of reality, but also to conceptualize the experiences of adverse groups by emphasizing common ground and by communicating in both directions' (Gray, 2008, 64). When scaled up from assessing individual works of music to tackling long-standing societal inequities and histories of violence or oppression, the tension between the commitments of peacebuilding as an activity that promises to effect radical positive change and the reality that accomplishing such change is a long, messy process marked not only by the scars of previous conflicts, but also by the establishment of new, conflictual relationships, becomes still more evident.

There is a fundamental idealism involved in thinking about societal change at any level, but if working in the field of music and conflict means pursuing work that, in Timothy Rice's words, will 'heal the wounds of loss and separation' (2017, 238), it is key that we understand the terms and processes through which we might be able to evaluate this healing. In this section I have surveyed a number of the methods, approaches, and literatures with the aim of clarifying how this nexus of music and conflict transformation has been discussed thus far. In the investigations that follow, I ask what we can actually discover about music's relationship to conflict transformation, and how that information can be best used to shape how we think through music and conflict. Central to this argument is the differentiation between the kinds of cultural 'work' done by different kinds of musical activities. I consider how music illuminates the intersection of multiple paradigms: those of empathy and guilt, of participatory and presentational performance, and of knowledge and acknowledgement. Throughout, I argue that one of the key features of musical activity as a catalyst for transforming conflict is its potential to invite its participants to acknowledge their moral responsibility for past wrongs. Given that studies in ethics, peacebuilding, and transitional justice regularly emphasise the importance of acknowledging individual and collective responsibility for wrongdoing (Barkan, 2000; Behrendt and Ben-Ari, 2012; Branscombe and Doosje, 2004; Gordy, 2013), music's facility for expressing negative emotions such as guilt and contrition would seem to play a central role in artistic responses to conflict. Instead, music has been overwhelmingly positioned as a vehicle for emotional catharsis, for facilitating social contact between opposing groups, and for fostering empathy and reconciliation. While each of these outcomes is a possible and indeed desirable feature of conflict transformation, the exclusive focus on these areas threatens to overly simplify narratives of how music might contribute to (or inhibit) the process of conflict transformation.

2 Constructing Transformation

2.1 Empathising with Others

We begin with a straightforward question: what *is* empathy? Though currently in vogue, as a word, empathy has a fairly short documented history in English: the most familiar narrative credits the psychologist Edward Titchener with coining the term in 1909 in order to translate Robert Vischer's nineteenth-century German neologism *Einfühlung* (literally, 'feeling into').[12] Vischer used Einfühlung/ empathy in the field of visual aesthetics to describe the human capacity for comprehending an artwork by projecting one's self into it; aesthetics would also provide many examples for Vischer's contemporary Theodor Lipps, a key exponent of Einfühlung/empathy as a broader philosophical category in the human and social sciences. Yet over the course of the twentieth century, this quality of aesthetic empathy grew to encompass a more interpersonal concept of empathy, familiar today as the capacity to participate vicariously in another person's perspective (cognitive empathy) and emotions (affective empathy). Various grounds for cognitive and affective empathy have been proposed, including influential work by Edith Stein (1989), at one time a student of the phenomenologist Edmund Husserl, who concluded that empathy is dependent on a perceived similarity between the empathiser and the empathised-with. Though these inflections of the term may be of relatively recent vintage, some aspects of this interpersonal empathy can be traced back further to the eighteenth-century philosophers Adam Smith and David Hume, who wrote of 'sympathy' and 'moral sentiments' as providing an explanation for how it is that we come to understand and to react to the emotions of another person.

In contemporary scholarship, the diversity of fields in which empathy has been studied is paralleled by the diversity of conceptions of what it is or does. As I suggest above, some think of empathy as arising from cognitive mechanisms related to perspective-taking, while others suggest it is a process of

---

[12] Some sources cite German philosopher Rudolf Hermann Lotze as using *Einfühlung* in 1858, but I have not been able to substantiate these claims. Meanwhile, Kirsty Martin (2013, 30 n.1) has argued (following the *Oxford English Dictionary*) that although Titchener's was the first published usage, Vernon Lee [Violet Paget] was the first to employ the English term 'empathy' in a diary entry dated 1904.

emotion-matching or affective 'contagion' (cf. Deutsch and Madle, 1975; Watt, 2007). In psychological and biocultural studies, empathy is studied both as a human trait ('dispositional' empathy) and as an induced state ('situational' empathy); cognitive scientists such as Evan Thompson (2001) argue for it as a central component of the individual human consciousness; while the ethnomusicologist Martin Stokes (2006, 2010) posits empathy as a social achievement within particular cultural contexts. Despite these varying interpretations about what constitutes empathy, there is a broad agreement – at least in the historically liberal West – that increasing reciprocal empathetic engagement and imaginative perspective-taking among either individuals or communities has the potential to address a wide variety of social crises and antagonisms arising in increasingly multicultural societies.

The lingering question is whether empathy can accomplish all that is required of it. When considering this it is notable that the positive view of empathy often entails a misappropriation of moral worth: in its fundamentals, cognitive empathy is morally neutral and even affective empathy is not necessarily morally good. Nonetheless, the moralistic inflection of empathy is supported by a growing discussion in the broader public sphere over the past few decades that regards empathy as a key human asset. Prominent figures, including Barack Obama, portray an 'empathy deficit' as a pressing human (and political) problem,[13] while psychologist Simon Baron-Cohen (2011) has argued that a lack of (in this case dispositional) empathy is at the root of human cruelty. With these claims, empathy is positioned as positive, universal, humanising, and teleologically oriented towards a society often vaguely defined as 'better' (more tolerant, less violent, etc.). This endows empathy with an amplified status that has been vigorously taken up within the organisations involved in conflict transformation – for example, by the Canadian-based charity Empathy for Peace, which describes empathy as an 'invaluable natural resource for conflict transformation' (2019, 4).

Following along with this surge in wider interest, scholars in a variety of social scientific fields have turned their attention to examining activities or situations that might increase empathy; in their turn, music scholars have made consistent links between music participation and increasing feelings of empathy, often

---

[13] Then-Senator Barack Obama (2006) discussed the 'empathy deficit' in his commencement address to graduates of Northwestern University on 19 June. Text and video available www .northwestern.edu/newscenter/stories/2006/06/barack.html (accessed 7 January 2020). More recently, former First Lady Michelle Obama (2020) referenced several disturbing moments in recent American public and political life as evidence of what happens when 'a total and utter lack of empathy [. . .] is ginned up into outright disdain'. Speech given 17 August 2020 at the Democratic National Convention. Transcript and video available https://wapo.st/2E6Z4rT (accessed 20 August 2020).

framed in terms of increasing openness to cultural 'others' or reconfiguring intergroup dynamics. For example, Eric Clarke suggests that, as 'a powerfully multisensory and particularly kinaesthetic phenomenon, whose embodied character draws people into fluid and powerful social groups at a range of scales and degrees of permanence and impermanence', music can 'enact a kind of empathy' (2019, 76). On an individual level, Tal-Chen Rabinowich and others have shown that musical group interactions increase empathy scores in children in ways 'that may extend beyond the realm of music to promote day-to-day emotional empathy' (Rabinowich, Cross, and Burnard, 2013, 494). Claims such as these have been buttressed further by empirical studies, including the project 'Music, Empathy, and Cultural Understanding' undertaken by Eric Clarke, Tia DeNora, and Jonna Vuoskoski, which produced what the authors call 'narrow but "hard-nosed" evidence for music's positive inter-cultural potential' in demonstrating that even passive listening to music can heighten empathetic responses in listeners with high dispositional empathy (2015a, 20; see also 2015b, 77). From other perspectives, the interaction of music and empathy has been studied in terms of the endocrinous opioid system and mirror neurons, the ethnomusicology of affect, and sociological studies of collective action. Although these studies stop short of claiming music as some kind of panacea for societal ills, they share the premise of musical participation changing social behaviour via affordances of compassionate insight and affiliation. The evidence they provide in support of this is suggestive, but on their own they do not attempt to answer the question of whether musically mediated empathy is the right or only tool to hand.

In tracing the promise of empathy within the context of music and conflict transformation, Laurence (2008, 14) suggests that music's 'specific potential to enable, catalyse and strengthen empathic response, ability and relationship' rests on the capacity for the activity of musicking to turn performance into a joint project through which participants strive to understand one another. The empathic responses such a project might generate offer a way for participants to accept difference as part of a 'thick' reconciliation process. Implicit in such a formulation is the willingness of participants to undertake this project of self-improvement, not to mention the presumption that expectations about what constitutes acceptable difference are (or can come to be) shared amongst group members. These obstacles aside, the consistency with which some scholars working on music and conflict employ similar, positive language to describe music's empathy-enhancing power in other post-conflict contexts suggests that there is something broadly appealing about this conception; certainly, musical projects that claim to bring together conflicting groups have frequently been the subject of widespread adulation (not to mention substantial funding).

In contrast, Arild Bergh takes a sceptical approach to the links between music, empathy, and conflict transformation. In his critique, he suggests that research on music in conflict transformation is weakened by 1) focusing on strong (peak) experiences; 2) employing an overly romantic view of music's capabilities; 3) evidencing the belief that non-rational interventions are likely to resolve conflict where rational approaches (i.e. addressing substantive social, economic, or ethnic issues) have failed; and 4) downplaying the reality of unequal power relations amongst participants, researchers, NGOs, and other interested parties (Bergh, 2011, 368). Bergh does not deny that music and empathy have roles to play in transforming conflict: in fact, he sees active, long-term musical participation and the empathy it can generate as possibly uniquely well-suited for certain kinds of transformation work. However, if we are to avoid slipping into the patterns of valorisation he exposes, we need to reconsider the standards by which we evaluate musical interventions in conflict transformation. By focusing on real-world contexts in which empathy might come into play, we can deepen the critique of empathy's role in musically mediated conflict transformation.

Questioning the capacity of empathy to contribute to conflict transformation is a provocation – it is hard to argue against the proposition (or aspiration) that 'greed is out, empathy is in', as Frans de Waal (2009, ix) put it. Nonetheless, the normative repercussions of the rush to empathise bear additional scrutiny. How can we avoid casting empathy as a universal virtue or music as (merely) a vehicle for empathy-driven social change? In part, perhaps, by paying close attention with Sara Ahmed (2004) to the ways in which emotions (to which empathy, of course, is closely related) and music are not politically neutral, but resonate within larger political landscapes. Given the potential for what Laurence (2008, 18) calls *negative* empathy, or the instrumentalisation of empathetic understanding as a tool of exploitation, perhaps also by rejecting a simple evaluation of empathy as morally good. In addition, we might look beyond empathy to examine how other facets of musical involvement might contribute to conflict transformation. To put the question more bluntly, if both the experience of particular emotions and their catharsis in a musical experience are susceptible to manipulation for particular political ends, what political work does the emphasis on music as empathy-enhancing do? – and what musical potential does it obscure?

Thinking about music's capacity to promote empathy and intergroup reconciliation in post-conflict societies clarifies the importance of such critique. This requires thinking not on what empathy *is*, but on what it *does*. Carolyn Pedwell (2014) suggests that empathy is, at its core, a technology of access: access to the experiences, feelings, and thoughts of others. (The parallels to the widespread

Western assumption that music makes the inner life – one's own or another's – available to interpretation are striking.) This epistemic function is central to transforming our conceptions of others, but considering empathy as a kind of personal or societal *technology* highlights two key features, namely, that empathic ability is not equally distributed and that the knowledge such technology yields is necessarily limited and fallible. Both urge discretion when it comes to the mobilisation of empathy as a relational tool.

Equally, thinking about empathy in terms of granting *access* to some facet of another's experience points our attention to a further cause for pause, in that access is linked to authority: the claim to have knowledge of the experience of another is close kin to the claim of an 'insider perspective' – and thus, a claim of authority over the truth about that experience. It is easy to imagine a situation in which persons who already possess power or privilege (and who are able to choose whether or not to empathise) claim authority over the experiences of the less powerful in order to shape the wider narrative to reinforce existing power structures. Any consideration of empathy thus involves questions of agency and motivation: who is empathising with whom and for what purpose?

The limits on the ability of empathy to overcome entrenched social divisions are also pertinent. These are encapsulated in its biases towards the *familiar* and the *here and now*. The former indicates that people tend to empathise more with those they know and who are similar to them (family, close friends, others who share core group identity characteristics, and so on), while the latter indicates that people empathise more with those present than those absent (see Hoffmann, 2000, esp. 62). This poses particular problems when individuals or groups distinguish themselves sharply from one another (as in entrenched beliefs about differing core characteristics) or are located far away from one another.[14] Empathy, then, seems to run into the same problems of scale noted previously in relation to music and conflict transformation in general.

Taken together, this suggests that empathy plays a complex and important role in developing not only our conceptions of one another but also our actions towards one another. It is a key part of moral development, and particularly the development of moral imagination. Yet, as Julinna Oxley (2011, 73–4) argues, it is not in itself sufficient for moral judgement, deliberation, or action. This is why in promoting empathy as a goal, it is often paired with ethical discourses that emphasise a radical identification with the 'Other' and its consequent intersubjective responsibility, derived from the work of Emmanuel Levinas (1969), or humanity's shared vulnerability and interdependency, drawn in part

---

[14] The importance of physical co-presence for the production of empathy has been debated, and may well be diminishing in the digitally shrunken world of the twenty-first century. Nevertheless, empathy seems to require a *perception* of closeness or similarity.

from the work of Judith Butler (2004, 2010).[15] Yet I remain sceptical that either
of these positions can adequately reflect the problems faced on the ground in
transforming conflict interventions.

One key problem with this ethical discourse hinges on the question of power
relations I raised with regard to empathy. Radical identification with and
responsibility towards the Other is a very different experience if one has
suffered at the hands of that Other than if one has had little contact with or
has occupied a position of power over the Other. For 'victims' an expectation of
the kind of openness promoted by Levinas and Butler may be both coercive and
cruel; for 'perpetrators' there may be pressures towards inappropriate emotions
such as pity or false empathy, while those in-between are likewise open to a
variety of unintended experiences. In what contexts is empathy precarious or
reliant on 'endless recitations of the ghastly and terrible' (Hartman, 1997, 4) that
might further alienate rather than reconcile? Moreover, the emphasis on vulnerability and openness is strikingly passive and interior in orientation. What
action is being taken is directed inwards towards confronting one's own vulner-
abilities and opening oneself up to new experiences. This solipsistic focus on
the self runs counter to the sense that empathy is something directed outwards
that can inspire action. How then can we translate this in those situations where
different groups will have suffered from conflict and all will be vulnerable, but
to vastly differing extents? To echo Ida Danewid (2017), is it really the case that
an ethics grounded in producing empathy on the basis of generalised suffering is
the best way to transform contemporary conflict?

I propose that music's capacity for inculcating empathy should be placed
within a simultaneously expanded and refined vision of music's relationship to
emotions, the moral imagination, and conflict transformation. In the sections
that follow, I argue in particular for a renewal of attention to how – in certain
contexts – music offers opportunities to acknowledge individual and collective
guilt and (often) to apologise for wrongs suffered by others as part of building
new kinds of communities. Music thus helps us to move beyond the problematic
discourse prevalent in conflict studies of 'victims' and 'perpetrators', or even
the more neutral 'participants', to consider the roles of individuals or groups
who do not fit neatly into these categories. This is especially important when
engaging with social structures or historic violence to which neither individual
guilt nor moral responsibility can be assigned. In situations where affective
relations between groups are marked by strongly hierarchical boundaries

---

[15] The term 'Other' has a distinguished philosophical history running from G. W. F. Hegel through
Edmund Husserl to Jacques Lacan and Levinas. I capitalise it in this section to indicate the
Levinasian take on self-other relations, whereas in other sections I prefer the unmarked 'other'.
For an example of how Levinasian thinking has been brought into music, see Warren (2014).

between those who are the *empathisers* and those who are being empathised *with*, such a musical acknowledgement of guilt can provide a necessary counterpart to empathy in reconfiguring existing social relations.

By investigating musical guilt in tandem with musical empathy, a more holistic picture of the constituent parts of conflict transformation emerges, as well as a clearer understanding of the wider contexts of music and potentially others of the arts within the field of conflict or peace studies. Thus, despite my critical stance towards some of the deployments of musical empathy, I do not reject musically mediated empathy as a key potential for transforming conflict; neither do I hold the acknowledgement of guilt as being of prior importance. Instead, considering how other-directed empathy and acknowledgement of guilt are woven together as complementary influences on moral formation gives us better tools with which to understand how music might transform conflict.

2.2 Expanding beyond Empathy

In contrast to the burgeoning literature on music and empathy, theorisations of guilt and music have a patchy intellectual history.[16] This is in spite of the central position of guilt as an ethically relevant interpersonal emotion, but it mirrors the relative lack of historical engagement between music and the larger field of ethics amongst both musicologists and ethicists.[17] In recent decades, the lacuna of music's relationship to ethics has begun to fill, and although disagreements about how and under what conditions music might possess moral force continue to shape scholarly discourse, a broad consensus has emerged that – at least in some circumstances – music, morality, and ethical principles can be productively linked.[18] Yet when we consider which musico-moral experiences have come under scholarly scrutiny, guilt remains an outlier. There are several potential reasons for this omission, including the links between guilt and legal processes and the resulting inference of a sharp distinction between guilt and innocence, its links to religious belief and theology, or its reliance on a discourse

---

[16] One area in which music and guilt have been studied in tandem is music and politics – particularly as related either to censorship or to the assessment of composers who have made suspect political choices. See, for example, Barrow (2011) and P. Hall (2018).

[17] For more on this lack of documented interest in music and ethics as well as some suggestions for ways forward, see Phillips-Hutton and Nielsen (in press).

[18] The alert reader will note a certain elision between ethics and morality here; this reflects both their shared origins derived from Greek and Latin synonyms (*moralis* and *ethikos*) and the overlap in their contemporary common usage. Some philosophers, notably Bernard Williams in *Ethics and the Limits of Philosophy* (2006), have sought to distinguish between the two, but no settled distinction exists. Because I am dealing with reasonably 'thin' interpersonal relations, I will focus on discussing moral implications following the differentiation offered by Avishai Margalit (2002, esp. 540–2). For more on the links between music, morality, and ethics, cf. Kivy (2009a, 2009b); Levinson (2015a); and Warren (2014).

of interpersonal responsibility. Looking beyond the individual, the controversy over the conceptual viability and practical repercussions of collective guilt is a further obstacle.

Although musically mediated guilt has not as yet fallen under the scholarly spotlight, there are multiple discussions of music and shame in both music studies and philosophical work (Levinson, 2015b; Party, 2009; on musical expression of emotions, see Putnam, 1987). In general, shame and guilt have been differentiated on the basis of their respective objects, which is to say that shame is a feeling about oneself as a person, while guilt is felt about one's actions. Shame's reliance on self-consciousness and a sense of exposure to others renders it at once a more intimate and often a more socially mediated emotion than guilt.[19] This intensified attention to the distinctive individual experience is why Ruth Leys suggests that shame has displaced guilt as the primary emotional referent in the West since the mid-twentieth century. On this reading, shame is particularly attractive to contemporary Western societies because 'it provides a technology for guaranteeing each individual's absolute difference from every other and does so in terms that avoid the moralisms associated with the theory of guilt' (Leys, 2007, 185).[20] While this analysis goes some way towards explaining shame's currency in the wider scholarly field, it is important to note that theories of shame and guilt have been developed in fields with differing relationships to music studies: guilt in political theory, criminology, and sociology; shame in psychology, anthropology, and gender studies. Shame has been developed by scholars more closely linked to music (especially the psychologist Silvan Tomkins [1995] and Eve Kosofsky Sedgewick [2003], a scholar of, among other things, gender studies and queer theory), while guilt as a theoretical concept has remained largely outside the purview of music scholars.

Quite apart from the familiar if terminologically problematic 'survivor's guilt', experiences of both guilt and shame are pervasive features of post-conflict societies, yet with a few exceptions (e.g. Pilzer, 2012) music scholars have said little about how either of these emotions are reflected in the music of these societies. Given how pivotal such experiences can be in terms of 'creating conditions of possibility for post-war reconciliation marked by political and moral transformation' (Lu, 2008, 369), this lack indicates that a renewed attention to these narratives has the potential to reconfigure our understanding

---

[19] In *Shame and Necessity* (1993), Bernard Williams argues that shame is at its core distress over the perceived failure to live up to one's own self-image rather than a result of what others may say or think about one's behaviour.

[20] Within cultural anthropology, the distinction between guilt and shame is overlaid with racial and cultural distinctions that can be traced back, in part, to Ruth Benedict (1946) and remain a lively source of discussion in that field.

of music in post-conflict society. In addition, the current prioritising of individual shame over either individual or collective guilt in music studies as a whole requires adjustment when we think about music and conflict. Research in social psychology has shown that guilt is more productive than shame when it comes to effecting change in interpersonal relationships (Lickel, Schmader, and Barquiassau, 2004, 50–1). Facilitating social transformation involves confronting actions and behaviours, while focusing on inner character – especially if the goal is to make one feel negatively about some immutable feature of one's disposition or situation – tends to generate defensive distancing and disengagement. Moreover, guilt is linked more closely with other-directed empathy and an acknowledgement of interdependence than is shame. As both an emotional response and a judgement of responsibility, guilt renews our attention to the relational character of conflict transformation. In particular, thinking through affective relations marked by guilt in post-conflict society points our attention to moral emotions as structuring elements of experience and as fleeting moments of affective potential for change. If acceptance of moral responsibility is made available through music, it can contribute to new affective relations between present audiences and past events or people that 'scramble assumptions of both temporal linearity and spatial self-containment' (Pedwell, 2014, 115), thereby expanding the horizon beyond the individual.

Guilt has potential to alter thinking about music and its communicative powers, but if music scholars are to reclaim guilt as a useful transhistorical concept, it will need to be reframed within a more capacious understanding of what it encompasses and how it can be put to use. To this end, one theoretical concept that is useful in analysing the role of musical guilt in transforming conflict is that of *implication*, or what Michael Rothberg (2019) calls the 'implicated subject'. In particular, the idea of implication highlights how individuals who are not directly responsible for causing harm might be productively brought into a conversation about the redress of historical or structural conflicts. By moving beyond the individualistic understanding of guilt and responsibility that underpin legal frames of justice while retaining the concept of both individual and collective moral responsibility, we can use implication to address legacies of conflict that extend beyond those immediately affected. As Rothberg notes, implication contains within it the sense of one's being 'folded into' events that are larger than the individual. This is a fundamentally relational concept: to take on the role of the implicated subject is to acknowledge one's relationship to other individuals, to larger communities, and to more complex histories. This is often a difficult or painful, but musical participation, with its capacity to inculcate feelings of oneness and to encourage empathy, is optimised for such an undertaking. Within music, this process of implication plays a significant role in drawing together disparate groups of people into a shared (if multi-voiced), musically mediated story.

2.3 Participation and Presentation

In his 2008 book *Music as Social Life: The Politics of Participation*, Thomas Turino identifies two major paradigms for real-time music-making.[21] The first, which he terms 'participatory', has the active contribution of many people to the music as its goal. This may include singing, clapping, dancing, playing, or other activities insofar as they are considered integral to the performance.[22] It is predicated on low to no distinctions between 'artist' and 'audience', and it prioritises shared interaction and social being over professionalised perform-ance quality. Many musical activities that might fall into the categories of community music, music therapy, or even public music, such as chanting at sports events, are participatory in nature, and the ideal of widespread participa-tion as a means of breaking down societal differences has popularised group participatory formats in musical conflict transformation efforts.

In contrast, 'presentational' music-making involves one group of people performing for another group. One readily apparent example is that of profes-sional musicians performing for an audience in a Western art music concert, but many other formats feature analogous separations between artist and audience (Turino discusses 'cosmopolitan' musical styles and the use of Indigenous dance for nationalist projects in Zimbabwe in some detail). This perceived separation between people based on different types of activity is one reason why these styles of music-making are less common than participatory models in music and conflict transformation projects. When they are invoked, it is often under the aegis of Western-oriented groups performing supposedly universal Western art music.

Turino's differentiation between performance styles is based on a distinction between what he calls 'the concept of a musical piece as a set item, an art object' in presentational culture and participatory culture's conception of a piece as 'a set of resources' (2008, 54). This has some commonality with performance studies scholar Diana Taylor's (2003) distinction between what she terms the 'archive' of knowledge as represented by material objects and a 'repertoire' of knowledge that is encapsulated in embodied practices, but both of these

---

[21] Turino also discusses two paradigms of recorded music ('high fidelity' and 'studio art'), but these are less relevant for my purposes here.

[22] Incidentally, this raises an interesting question about the function of non-integral participation (or interjection). For example, the infamous incident when a disgruntled fan called the newly electrified Bob Dylan 'Judas' was certainly not integral to Dylan's performance in 1966, yet it has become a key moment for how we retroactively understand Dylan's 1966 performance.

dichotomies are difficult to maintain in practice. For example, Turino argues that participatory music has traditionally been seen as an informal or amateur style of music-making and has been accorded less prestige than its presentational counterpart, but he claims that it 'connects people more intimately and power-fully [than presentational style music-making] because of shared interactive engagement among all participants in the *actual doing* of the activities with each other' (2008, 61–2). This shared engagement increases the sense of oneness with other participants – a process Turino calls 'sonic bonding'.[23] Yet, it is not clear that such developments are unique to participatory styles. The musicologist Nicholas Cook (2013, 319–24) has argued that listening to music is intrinsically an active, embodied process that allows for many of the same social processes as participatory performance; recall also that the Clarke, DeNora, and Vuoskoski study mentioned previously found changes in empathy based on individual listening to recorded music (a paradigm far removed from Turinian participa-tion). This suggests that the strict separation Turino enacts between participatory and presentational styles is unsustainable: a more expansive vision of participa-tion that takes note of the roles of those we might term 'users' (audiences and attendees), 'performers' (artists and producers), and 'stewards' of music (all those in supporting roles) in both live and recorded contexts will be more representative of how music actually works in contemporary practice.

Whether music is considered to be participatory, presentational, both, or neither, the ideal of musical encounters with others resulting in transformational change demands careful handling to avoid overstatement. Consider, for example, the blurring of boundaries of participation and presentation, self and other in one of the best-known endeavours in musical conflict transformation: the West–Eastern Divan Orchestra. The orchestra was founded in 1999 by Daniel Barenboim and Edward Said as evidence of the conductor/pianist and cultural theorist/literary critic's 'hope to replace ignorance with education; to humanize the other; to imagine a better future'.[24] The ensemble's lofty goals are picked up in Western media accounts of their performances: amongst British newspapers, Alexandra Coghlan (2014) proclaims 'the symbolism of Daniel Barenboim's West–Eastern Divan Orchestra has never been more potent or necessary' in an *Independent* review; George Hall (2015) notes that they are 'uniquely inspiring' for the *Guardian*; while in an early assessment *The*

---

[23] Turino's argument has a strong resemblance to anthropological discussions of ritual behaviour, especially Victor Turner's (1969) idea of *communitas*.

[24] This description featured prominently on the West–Eastern Divan Orchestra's website until December 2019 (see https://bit.ly/2YgScih); at the time of writing, the current website dispenses with the multi-lingual layout and with this rationale, instead focusing heavily on the West–Eastern Divan's projects in Berlin, their worldwide performance tours, and opportunities for financial support.

Observer (2006) declares that 'here is peaceful collaboration in action; young people from communities which, though apparently hopelessly divided, have come together to make music'. In a parallel stamp of approval, the United Nations designated the West–Eastern Divan Orchestra as a Global Advocate for Cultural Understanding in 2016 on the basis that 'the work of the Orchestra is testimony to the power of music to break down barriers and to build bridges between communities' (United Nations, 2016).

Prominent musical undertakings headlined by superstar musicians generate headlines, but when it comes to evidence of this musical coming-together actually transforming cultural engagement, the picture becomes less clear. Twenty years on from its founding, the general sanguinity characterising the reception of the West–Eastern Divan Orchestra flies in the face of the seemingly intractable conflict in Israel/Palestine, Europe, and the wider Arab world from which the musicians are drawn. Yet, 'humaniz[ing] the other' is only one of the ensemble's goals, and despite the continued framing of the orchestra in political terms, its political power is necessarily constrained; perhaps it is unfair to take it to task for its failure to transform an entire geopolitical region. More pertinent, perhaps, is the West–Eastern Divan Orchestra as a warning against overzealous expectations of radical change. Indeed, recent descriptions of the orchestra's work on its website are more modest, focusing on music's potential to '[grant] the individual the right and obligation to express herself or himself fully while listening to his or her neighbour'. The emphasis on individual rights (and the concurrent separation of individuals and the communities from which they come) is striking; so too, is the lack of any explicit expectation of engagement. In other words, because self-expression is paramount one has an obligation to listen to one's neighbour but not – necessarily – to engage meaningfully with what is expressed. In a later section, the orchestra itself is held up as 'an alternative model [for ...] the Middle East' that is based on 'notion[s] of equality, cooperation and justice for all'.[25] This positioning steps back from the optimism of the orchestra's early days, but it nonetheless demonstrates what scholars such as Rachel Beckles Willson have argued is a 'legacy of nineteenth-century European idealism, and often a conviction that the symphony orchestra can transcend some of the dilemmas of an alarmingly fractured world' (Beckles Willson, 2013, 3; see also Beckles Willson, 2009) that may not be reflected in the day-to-day experiences of the musicians.

Equally as concerning from the perspective of those involved in music as a means of transforming conflict in Israel/Palestine is that the acclaim accorded to

---

[25] The West–Eastern Divan Orchestra, west-eastern-divan.org/divan-orchestra (accessed 7 January 2020).

the West–Eastern Divan Orchestra draws funding and opportunities away from local organisations in both the Middle East and in Spain where the orchestra rehearses each summer; as an institution, the orchestra largely reinvests its considerable financial and cultural capital in Europe and North America (of the seven 'Partner Projects' listed on its website, only one, 'Barenboim-Said for Music, Ramallah', is actually located in the Middle East).[26] For the performers themselves, these European links are more professionally beneficial than those to Israel/Palestine or the wider Middle East, particularly as the region has faced extreme instability in the past decade.[27] Even if collaborative ensemble music-making has the potential to create what Benjamin Brinner (2009, 326) calls 'a model of how one might live together not only in peace, but also in mutually beneficial harmony',[28] the question of whether those who participate in the West–Eastern Divan Orchestra return to their homes (or indeed, to homes or careers in Europe or North America) after the workshops, concerts, and tours with permanently changed attitudes towards a cultural 'other' is not only difficult to answer but also reflects a suspiciously one-sided vision of music as intrinsically edifying.

The potential problems of imposed cultural hierarchies and limited political efficacy aside, the West–Eastern Divan Orchestra and other similar projects do offer opportunities for sustained contact and collaborative engagement – perhaps even transmission of repertorial knowledge – between members of groups locked in conflict. Their potential for transforming conflict is predicated on an essentially participatory model in which musicians work alongside one another and – crucially – listen to one another in the heightened manner necessary for high-level musical performance. In the case of the West–Eastern Divan Orchestra, the performance conventions of Western art music means that the narrowly participatory aspect is unavailable to their audiences; nevertheless, the vision of social harmony they project in their performances is explicitly positioned as a didactic example for audience members to follow. This suggests

---

[26] The West–Eastern Divan Orchestra, 'Partner Projects', https://west-eastern-divan.org/partner-projects (accessed 7 January 2020). The three charitable foundations listed (registered in Spain, Germany, and the USA) also contribute to projects in the Middle East without giving further information.

[27] In 2020, the audition website notes that applicants 'should have a national background of any country from the Middle East, North Africa or Spain'; Beckles Willson (2009, 331–2) notes that from 2007 this background was defined as a blood relative of up to the second degree, rendering anyone with a grandparent from one of these countries eligible. Although current information about players is not publicised, in 2006 a number of performers identified more strongly with their European ties (both personal and professional) than their Middle Eastern heritage.

[28] Brinner's focus is on local efforts in Israel-Palestine, particularly the work of the bands Alei Hayazit and Bustam Abraham and the Iraqi Jewish performer Yair Dalal. He notes that because they draw on Middle Eastern idioms in a near-popular musical style, they avoid the re-inscription of Western European cultural hierarchies implied by Western art music.

that while scepticism over the efficacy of one-off concerts (often of Western musical styles and headlined by Western musical celebrities) is well-founded, enforcing a division between participatory and presentational music may ultimately be of limited use in theorising about music and conflict. This is all the more so if it is accompanied by a moralistic inflection of one as inherently better than the other. Both of these performance paradigms (not to mention performances that exist along the continuum that links them) encourage specific forms of identity formation and feelings of social solidarity, but they achieve this 'sonic bonding' in different ways. Acting together in making music contributes to feelings of unity for participants, while for presentational style music, 'group bonds are particularly channelled through the presentational performers rather than each member of the group's focusing on each other directly through dancing and making musical sound together' (Turino, 2008, 62). This diverse channelling of identification has significant repercussions for the nurturing of empathy and moral responsibility. Thus, even though I do not adopt Turino's semiotic interpretation of performance or the sharply drawn distinction between participatory and presentational music, thinking about the differences in social meaning that are produced through musical performance is a key means of framing music's contribution to transforming conflict.

2.4 Locating Music within Conflict Transformation

Drawing together these themes, I propose the following outline for organising thinking about the process of conflict transformation and for locating music's role within it. The transformational process has four overlapping stages, each of which contains its own societal challenges:

- Truth
- Acknowledgement
- Restitution
- Reconstitution

It is important to note that each of these abstractions covers a broad range of potential activities related to conflict transformation. The first, *truth*, refers to the process of establishing (insofar as is possible) the facts about what caused the conflict and what happened during the conflict. *Acknowledgement*, as I suggest above, refers to the process of transferring these facts into an accepted (if not always equally or experientially *shared*) narrative. This normally involves two separate actions, namely, the affirmation of factual truth and acknowledgement of responsibility in some form. *Restitution* is the restoration, or making good of previous wrongs (whether such acts are symbolic or material), and *reconstitution* is the negotiation of a new kind of relationship between the parties who have been in conflict.

Music has the potential to be influential at each of these stages, but in the two sections that follow, I focus on two specific examples of music's contributions to factual acknowledgement through consciousness-raising and invocations of moral responsibility. The first example ('Sorry Song') comes from Australia, and the second (*The Secret Path*) from Canada. Each is part of society-wide efforts at achieving transitional justice in those countries in relationship to the conflicts between white settler-colonists and Indigenous peoples, and each draws on elements of empathy and guilt in broadcasting knowledge, building acknowledgement, and encouraging moral responsibility regarding these conflicts. In particular, I focus on their ability to encourage the adoption of what, following Rothberg, I term implicated subject positions through presenting opportunities for communal apology or symbolic identification. In each case, I sketch out the respective historical contexts of the conflict and recent reconciliation efforts before analysing the musical examples and their performances in more detail.

3 Singing Sorry

In Australia, the transitional justice movement has taken as its primary subject the separation of Aboriginal, Torres Strait Islander, and mixed-race Australian children from their families and communities between the late nineteenth century and the 1970s.[29] At the time, these removals were often rationalised in terms of child welfare, but the belief that children of mixed descent could be successfully assimilated into white Australian society and that doing so would hasten the dwindling of the Indigenous population led to widespread racial profiling. Most children removed from their communities were sent to boarding schools (usually run by religious organisations), but in some cases, children (particularly those of mixed-race descent) were fostered by white families and raised in purposeful ignorance of their heritage (HREOC, 1997). First termed the 'Stolen Generations' in a pamphlet written in 1981 by historian Peter Read (2006), the moniker has become a rallying point for political activists concerned with historical abuse, lingering social inequality, and widespread injustice. Although aspects of the history of the Stolen Generations remain controversial, it is clear that such removals weakened family and tribal structures and contributed to social breakdown in ways that continue to reverberate in Indigenous society.

---

[29] Note that 'Aboriginal' refers to those Indigenous peoples whose countries, or ancestral territories, are in mainland Australia, while 'Torres Strait' refers to those whose countries are in the islands of the Torres Strait. I use 'Indigenous Australian' to refer to both groups.

In response to pressure for an investigation into the history of Indigenous child removals, the Australian government commissioned an inquiry under the auspices of the Human Rights and Equal Opportunity Commission (HREOC) in 1995. This was preceded by a series of key moments in Australian political history, including the 1967 referendum that amended the Constitution to include Indigenous peoples in the Australian census as citizens, the landmark *Mabo v Queensland (No. 2)* high court judgement in 1992 that rejected the doctrine of *terra nullius* and acknowledged native land title in Australia, and then-Prime Minister Paul Keating's emotive acknowledgement of the impact of the settlers' arrival in his 1993 'Redfern' speech.[30] In the 'Community Guide' accompanying HREOC's final report, entitled *Bringing Them Home* and published on 26 May 1997, the Commission summarised their findings by acknowledging

> Indigenous families and communities have endured gross violations of their human rights. These violations continue to affect Indigenous people's daily lives. They were an act of genocide, aimed at wiping out Indigenous families, communities and cultures, vital to the precious and inalienable heritage of Australia. (HREOC, 2002, 14)

They also called upon the government to record Indigenous testimonies of forced removal, to fund the relevant committees tasked with carrying out the recommendations, and to make reparation to those affected by forcible removal, defined by the report as including 'acknowledgement and apology', 'guarantees against repetition', 'measures of restitution [. . . and] rehabilitation', and 'monetary compensation' (HREOC, 2002, 15). Since the 1990s, progress has sometimes been slow: the federal government would take another decade before offering a formal apology in a speech given by then-Prime Minister Kevin Rudd on 13 February 2008 ('Apology to Australia's Indigenous Peoples'). However, in addition to these official recommendations, the report suggested that an official day be set aside for communities to acknowledge the impact of forced removals. In contrast to the government action, this proved to be quicker to implement: in 1998, a coalition of community groups took the suggestion forward in what

---

[30] *Terra nullius* [no man's land] is an official designation under international law that signifies a territory that is not claimed by any state or to which the previous sovereign has relinquished sovereignty. The application of *terra nullius* in Australia meant that the settlers did not make treaties with the Indigenous peoples regarding land or other rights, but rather claimed the land outright, with the result that disputes over land use became the basis of numerous court cases from the early nineteenth century. The *Mabo* judgement held that native customs, including land claims, were not superseded by English law. Keating's 'Redfern' speech took place in Redfern Park in New South Wales at the launch of the 1993 International Year of the World's Indigenous People. In it, Keating acknowledged, 'We took traditional lands and smashed the traditional way of life. We brought the diseases. The alcohol. We committed the murders. We took the children from their mothers. We practised discrimination and exclusion.' Transcript available at https://bit.ly/3gcyxX4 (accessed 7 January 2020).

would become an annual commemorative event held on 26 May known initially as National Sorry Day (renamed National Healing Day in 2005). Annual commemorations of the National Apology in February and National Sorry/Healing Day in May – as well as the official Reconciliation Week which follows the latter, from 27 May to 3 June – join older initiatives such as NAIDOC (National Aborigines and Islanders Day Observance Committee) Week as important landmarks in Australia's ongoing journey towards reconciliation; however, it is the opportunity these officially sanctioned events provide for Australians to perform acts of apology, forgiveness, and reconciliation that is of immediate relevance.

Music, and especially song, has played a significant role within these various initiatives, from consciousness-raising popular songs such as 'Took the Children Away' by Archie Roach, public-facing performances such as that of 'Treaty' by Yothu Yindi and 'Beds are Burning' by Midnight Oil at the Closing Ceremony of the Sydney Olympics in 2000, to the use of Aboriginal songs as evidence of native title in court cases.[31] Yet amongst many other efforts, Kerry Fletcher's 'Sorry Song' stands out as a means of performing reconciliation in Australia by virtue of its strong associations with official symbols of reconciliation and its clarity of message. A white Western Australian musician and Indigenous rights activist, Fletcher composed 'Sorry Song' in 1998 to address two audiences: it was 'written for the Stolen Generations of Aboriginal Australians and Torres Strait Islanders and dedicated to all First Nations people whose lives have been affected by the policy of Indigenous Child Removals', but at the same time it is for 'all of us whose hearts ache when we think of the pain those children and communities suffered and the pain which they still endure today'.[32] Its premiere took place on the first-ever National Sorry Day, 26 May 1998, and it remains a feature of many musical performances both on National Sorry/Healing Day and at other points during the annual National Reconciliation Week.

In terms of its formal structure, 'Sorry Song' is straightforward, yet adaptable. Fletcher's original lyrics were divided into three brief verses interspersed with a simple chorus; after the government's Apology in 2008, Fletcher modified the song to include another verse and chorus sung to the same melody as the original text, thereby reflecting the perceived importance of the government's actions in promoting reconciliation (see Figure 1).

---

[31] The use of song and sacred objects as evidence was famously part of the Yolngu people's petition to the Supreme Court of the Northern Territory in 1971. Although the *Milirrpum* decision ruled against them on the basis of *terra nullius*, this paved the way for later cases that established native title in part through evidence of ritual occupation and use. See also Koch and Crowe (2013). For more information about the role of popular music in Australia over this time period, see Corn (2011).

[32] Kerry Fletcher, 'Sorry Song', description available on www.philipgriffin.com/sorrysong (accessed 7 January 2020).

Verse 1
If we can now say that we're sorry to the people from this land.
Verse 2
They cry, they cry, their children were stolen, they still wonder why.
Chorus 1
Sing, sing loud, break through the silence. Sing 'sorry' across this land.
Verse 3
We cry, we cry, their children were stolen, now no-one knows why.
Chorus 1 (repeat)
Sing, sing loud, break through the silence. Sing 'sorry' across this land.
Verse 4 (added 2008)
We sing with our hearts, 'Respect for each and ev' ryone, together, with hope burning
   strong'
Chorus 2 (added 2008)
Sing, sing loud, we've broken the silence. Let 'sorry' start healing our land

---

Figure 1 'Sorry Song' lyrics, written by Kerry Fletcher. Used by
permission.

The performance format is flexible, with varying notated and recorded versions for solo voice or mixed chorus, and featuring different numbers of repeats in circulation. This is emphasised by the accessible, popular-style musical accompaniment that harmonises the melody with just three chords (I, IV, and V, or C major, F major, and G major in the published score) that can likewise be performed by a variety of instruments.

This simplicity of construction contributes to the song's prominence: in addition to featuring regularly in commemorative reconciliatory events and in choral repertoires, it was selected for inclusion in the 2007 edition of *Sing!*, an educational resource aimed at primary school-age children across Australia, and has featured in educational materials on Australian Studies in Germany.[33] Examples of the didactic use of 'Sorry Song' can be found in YouTube videos showing groups of students spelling out 'Sorry' on a field or showing the hands of a child slowly unfolding to reveal palms emblazoned with the Aboriginal symbol of the hibiscus, or desert rose, and the words 'sorry today' painted on her fingertips (see Figure 2 for a photo of one of these efforts); in these videos, the musical accompaniment of 'Sorry Song' frames the message of the physical gestures.[34]

---

[33] *Sing!* 1975–2014 Song Index. The index has been archived by the Australian Broadcasting Company, but can be viewed via the Wayback Machine at https://bit.ly/3hdRwBL (accessed 7 January 2020); see also Rickwood (2013,10–11).

[34] Butupa, 'National Sorry Day 2015, Australia Giant Human SORRY, Australia says sorry', YouTube video, 2'34", 8 February 2008, www.youtube.com/watch?v=bhYPfsDB-LA (accessed

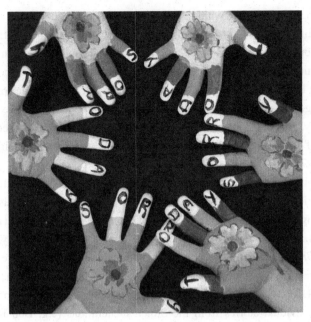

Figure 2 Photo showing hands painted with the words 'Sorry Today'. Image courtesy of Mark Binns.

Like the government's apology itself, Fletcher's composition has not been uncontroversial, particularly in its educational usage. In 2007, one school in New South Wales banned the song after a parent complained of inappropriate political indoctrination (Tobin, 2007). At the heart of the issue was the song's moral implications: specifically, its support for apologising to Indigenous Australians and the concomitant acknowledgement of the extent to which present societies are implicated in the past actions of others. Although cloaked in the language of political choices, these are essentially concerns over how to apportion (or indeed teach) moral responsibility. This echoes wider anxieties about how to teach Australian history, and particularly criticism of what is known as the 'black armband view of history', a view which former Prime Minister John Howard characterised as reproducing 'a belief that most Australian history since 1788 has been little more than a disgraceful story of imperialism, exploitation, racism, sexism and other forms of discrimination'.[35] Like many reconciliatory efforts,

7 January 2020); Butupa, 'National Sorry Day 2015-"Sorry Song" Australia', YouTube video, 1'11", 8 February 2008, www.youtube.com/watch?v=xvRFvSt3JAA (accessed 7 January 2020).

[35] The 'black armband of history' is a phrase originating with historian Geoffrey Blainey in the 1993 Sir John Latham Memorial Lecture; John Howard's explanation is taken from the 1996 Sir Robert Menzies Lecture 'The Liberal Tradition: The Beliefs and Values Which Guide the Federal Government.' Text available https://bit.ly/3l0HyWT (accessed 7 January 2020).

'Sorry Song' thus operates within a heavily politicised milieu wherein a divisive discourse of collective guilt (frequently glossed as national shame) contributes to a contentious public sphere. Nonetheless, Fletcher herself claims that it is not political but personal: in commenting on the New South Wales ban she told the Australian Broadcasting Company 'it concerns me that some people are reading political agendas into this song, when the song is about personal tragedy in our community. I've witnessed the confusion and pain that were caused by the removal of children, and I think this song speaks of an important truth' (qtd. in Tobin, 2007).

In pivoting from 'political agendas' to claiming truth as part of the song's concern, Fletcher not only asserts a moral stance for her work but also aligns 'Sorry Song' with the reconciliatory aims of extending knowledge and acknowledgement. Here, 'Sorry Song' reflects the imperative of testimony evident from the *Bringing Them Home* inquiry, which asserted that 'giving testimony, while extraordinarily painful for most, is often the beginning of the healing process' (HREOC, 1997, 17). Unlike other examples of reconciliatory music that tell individual stories from the Stolen Generations (e.g. Bob Randall's 'Brown Skin Baby [They Took Me Away]') or make specific requests for governmental or public action (e.g. Fletcher's own 'Let's Recognise', which agitates for further changes to Australia's Constitution), 'Sorry Song' focuses on the acknowledgement of the general experience of family separations. It affirms the value of individual victims sharing their experiences and even encourages communities to make additional gestures of apology or reconciliation outside of a musical context, yet in this piece Fletcher tellingly avoids any comment on what other elements (for instance, monetary compensation) might be considered as part of reconciliation. She also sidesteps the question of whether or not non-Indigenous Australians should feel a sense of collective guilt over the Stolen Generations. Instead, she chooses to focus on apologies refracted through song: acts that can be taken up by both individuals and communities without demanding an acceptance of moral responsibility for the past.

A closer examination of the song's lyrics reveals additional tensions over the individual and communal reckoning with the experiences of the Stolen Generations. The text emphasises the hesitancy and shared difficulty of speaking about the past, both for those who have suffered and those who are presently in the position of offering the song's titular apology. Both truth and acknowledgement initially seem far away, and it is only through acts of empathy that the presumably non-Indigenous speakers come to acknowledge their implication in past abuse. By saying 'sorry', they release everyone from the tyranny of silence and bring healing to the land. Yet in this context of mutual healing and reconciliation, it is striking that the lyrics themselves are essentially one-sided in their evocation of identity and assignment of agency. In the first three verses, the consistent opposition between first- and third-person language implies a division between an Indigenous 'they' and a non-Indigenous 'we' that reinforces the perception of Indigenous experience as being 'other' to that of non-Indigenous Australians. From its inception, then, there is a conflict over who gets to be 'we' that comes uncomfortably close to reinforcing the idea that the truest 'we' in Australia are in fact the white settler-colonists and their descendants.[36] Furthermore, the song maintains a separation of Australian society into those who are helpless in the face of power ('they cry', 'they still wonder why') and those who, by virtue of the magnanimous gesture of apologising, can bring healing to the nation.[37] This is emphasised when, in a striking instance of lyrical empathetic identification (a less generous interpretation might suggest a certain level of appropriation), the emotional devastation of the break-up of families visited upon the Indigenous community in verse two is transferred in verse three to the (implicitly non-Indigenous) 'we' who cry over the fate of those families. Although 'Sorry Song' stems from a desire to promote apology and reconciliation, it nevertheless contains traces of a problematic identitarian discourse.

The implicit racialised nature of the lyrics' social divisions is particularly surprising given that the performance ideal for 'Sorry Song' is that of community music: local choirs or groups of schoolchildren singing together, many of which would include participants of Indigenous heritage (as we shall see shortly, this is the case in one of the most iconic performances of 'Sorry Song'). One reasonable counterargument is to suggest that the focus on non-Indigenous Australian experience is a natural result of the song's existence within a frame of apology, itself an overture made by non-Indigenous towards Indigenous peoples in Australia. As a song written by and on behalf of white settler-colonist Australians, the tension between 'we' and 'they' accentuates the way past experience continues to divide present society even as the lyrics and performance traditions hold out a hope for a future collective that encompasses Indigenous and non-Indigenous Australians alike. Furthermore, the lyrical division into ethnic groups is erased in the fourth verse when the key value of

---

[36] It also echoes the challenges around defining harm-causing and apology-offering groups – for example, the debate around the responsibility of the national government (as ostensibly representative of all Australians, Indigenous and not) to apologise to some Australians on behalf of other Australians or that around the responsibility of recent immigrants (more than 25 per cent of Australia's population, many of whom are non-white, are foreign-born) to Australia. For more on the operation of various collectivities in Australia, see McGarty and Bliuc (2004).

[37] As one of the anonymous readers of this text commented, there is perhaps a faint echo here of the paternalism characteristic of the 1984 Band Aid single 'Do They Know It's Christmas?'

respect for every person is propagated by the act of all Australians singing together. In this sense there are two different kinds of 'we' present in the song: the non-Indigenous Australian 'we' whose act of apology allows them to come together with (or absorb?) their Indigenous counterparts into a new and non-racialised Australian 'we'. The implicit ideal of eventual unity is admirable; nonetheless, in the context of continuing arguments over the best ways to address Australia's legacy of racial discrimination, any structures that privilege the experience and emotional perspective of non-Indigenous Australians should raise questions regarding the power relationships between Indigenous and non-Indigenous peoples that continue to have an impact on Australian society.

It is tempting to interpret this apology song as offering a paradigmatic moment of interpersonal identification in which largely non-Indigenous audiences and performers are guided through the acknowledgement of Indigenous experience with the aim of increasing empathy for those who remain culturally 'other'. Yet in performance, the frame of apology enclosing 'Sorry Song' offers a double-layered enactment that stretches beyond the empathy with which it begins. In its first layer, participants are asked to engage empathetically with others in their immediate surroundings. This is fundamentally an embodied phenomenon, though it can be expressed in terms of physical gesture, for instance by standing in respect or joining hands, or in terms of performance, as in features of choral singing such as collective breathing and harmonic listening. Nicholas Cook (1998, 75) goes so far as to suggest that such enactment of community is a function of all choral performances, and the implicit inclusion of the entire audience as participants in this kind of empathy casts this performance in the mould of participatory music-making.

In addition to the bringing-together the song effects in the physical nature of its performance, the shift in the final verse and chorus to a simple 'we' enacts a symbolic reconciliation: the underlying harmonies reflect this closure with a conventional move back to the tonic. This reconciliation, however, is built upon an implicit moral stance of implication. Rehabilitating the Australian 'we' into an integrated collective requires not only including the experiences of the 'they' in the overall narrative, but also the acknowledgement of non-Indigenous complicity in that experience. This implication is accessed through a shared affective response to the child removals: a response that is afforded in large part by the empathetic identification engendered in performance. The damage caused by child removals and the myriad other abuses suffered by Indigenous peoples is not healed through language; rather, it is the emotive crying of Indigenous peoples that becomes the fount of healing words. Fletcher's 'Sorry Song' makes the connection explicit in that before the non-Indigenous singers are able to sing 'together with hope burning strong' with their Indigenous counterparts they must first weep with them over the wrongs of the past. This empathetically motivated enactment of communal reconciliation is predicated on an acknowledgement on the part of the non-Indigenous participants of their implication in those particular histories and their shared moral responsibility for the violence of the past. This is, after all, an apology song.

Given that it is structured as a conversational address between two specific groups of people, it might be argued that 'Sorry Song's' most effective mode of existence is not as an enduring musical 'work' (in the sense of being codified in a score), but as repertorial knowledge: an embodied practice of apology performed in real time and transmitted via gesture and singing. With this in mind, let us examine a key performance of 'Sorry Song' as an example of how this performed apology might have worked at a particular moment in time.

On 13 February 2008, community choir Madjitil Moorna appeared onstage in Wellington Square in Perth, Western Australia, as part of a public celebration of the prime minister's apology to Indigenous Australians. Following spoken introductions, the choir launched into their first piece accompanied by a single guitar: a four-and-a-half-minute performance of 'Sorry Song' in its original three-verse format (see Figure 3). In video footage of the event, the audience responds as the choir begins to sing by rising to their feet; from 2'10" to 2'15" on the video, it is possible to hear an audience member comment 'be upstanding ... and upstanding we are'.[38] They remain standing throughout the choir's

Figure 3 Photo of Madjitil Moorna performing 'Sorry Song', 13 February 2008. Photo by Peter Randell, used by permission. Video of performance available online.

---

[38] This video was later uploaded to YouTube, www.youtube.com/watch?v=4s93lxO3yBQ (accessed 1 July 2020). A second video of this performance, with slightly different timings is available at www.youtube.com/watch?v=eKHExD3slR4 (accessed 1 July 2020); a copy of this footage, together with other events of the day, is held in the State Library of Western Australia.

performance, which extends the standard three-verse structure by repeating several elements and including a bridge containing the words 'one day, one day' sung in three-part harmony. As the song moves to its conclusion a few minutes later the choir moves forward with gently swaying outstretched arms, encouraging the audience to join in. The audience oblige by mirroring the choir's behaviour (roughly 6'10"–6'36"), although the audio quality is not high enough to determine how many actually sing. The choir continue singing in a near-incantatory fashion, eventually coming to a halt after seven repetitions of the chorus. As the song ends, the audience applauds wildly, ending the performance with the rather incongruous visual juxtaposition of behaviour associated with a sort of musical ecstasy engendered at concerts and the low-key performance style of the choir.

This musical performance of sung apology is framed by multiple spoken introductions: first by Bringing Them Home Committee (Western Australia) co-convenor the Reverend Dr Ian Robinson, then by human rights activist and long-time choir member Robyn Slarke.[39] From the initial welcome speech, the tone of the performance is one of respect and celebration: Slarke begins by welcoming the 'elders, members of the Stolen Generations, distinguished guests, citizens, activists, and friends', and bursts of applause punctuate both speeches. As Slarke's introduction continues, she speaks directly to those of Indigenous heritage in a noteworthy address that sheds some light on how the performance of 'Sorry Song' was perceived by choir members, saying: 'On this momentous day, we are honoured to sing and to bear witness to you, the Stolen Generations and your families, and all First Nations peoples whose lives have been torn apart by the policy of indigenous child removals.' As a non-Indigenous representative of a mixed-ethnicity choir speaking to a mixed-ethnicity audience, Slarke's division between 'we' and 'you' invokes performance as an opportunity for bilateral communication that involves everyone, regardless of ethnic heritage. Moreover, the impulse to bear witness to the suffering of Australia's Indigenous community through music frames 'Sorry Song' as both a gesture of apology offered by one social group to another and as an opportunity for members of choir and audience to reach across the social divisions that separate Australian society and sing together.

This interpretation of 'Sorry Song' is strengthened by choir Madjitil Moorna's well-known commitment to bringing together non-Indigenous and Indigenous people in performance. Billed as 'singers of Noongar [the local

---

[39] Bringing Them Home Committee (Western Australia) is an activist group 'working towards the recognition and healing of the pain caused by the removal of Aboriginal and Torres Strait Islander children from their families.' 'Bringing Them Home (WA): Aims and Objectives', https://bringingthemhomewa.com/aims-objectives/ (accessed 7 January 2020).

Aboriginal people in Perth] songs', Madjitil Moorna comprises both Indigenous and non-Indigenous Australians, including some members with personal experience of the Stolen Generations. The choir reflects its community origins in appearance and demeanour. The singers in this video are attired all in black clothes with yellow scarves bearing Aboriginal symbols (a deliberate reference to the Aboriginal flag); though the marked preference for short-sleeved or sleeveless tops is likely a concession to the summer heat, the lack of standardisation and general informality of dress creates the impression that choir members have worn everyday clothes. For this performance in Perth, the group was joined by five primary school-age children and their teacher who sing alongside the choir whilst performing in Australian Sign Language.

It may be easy to dismiss the musical euphoria seen during this performance (along with Slarke's claim for Madjitil Moorna as a powerful force for change in her prefatory remarks) as naïve emotionalism driven by the 'high' of a significant political victory, but this video nevertheless demonstrates how the performative apology in 'Sorry Song' can be framed as a means of (at least temporary) reconciliation between social groups as communities join together. It is a single performance lasting less than ten minutes from the beginning of the speeches until the end of the song, yet it is difficult not to be struck by the physical expression of emotion in the choir and audience that is evident even from the distance engendered by watching an amateur video. If the revelation and (eventual) healing of trauma is linked to the combination of language and music in generating affective empathy, claiming moral responsibility, and offering apology, it seems clear that the impulse to involve the body as part of a community through movement and song can be a powerful mediator of reconciliation following traumatic experience.

In performance, 'Sorry Song' aims to bring together groups of people (often, as in Perth, in racially mixed contexts) to stimulate greater cultural understanding through the acknowledgement of different and traumatic histories and the negotiation of local, contingent versions of what it means to apologise. The process of acknowledging one's moral implication in the suffering of others is complicated – especially in the context of the communal relationships enacted in 'Sorry Song'. In part this has to do with its relationship to the contested past of Australia and of the Stolen Generations, which is recognised, though not explored, in the lyrics of 'Sorry Song'. However, it is also partially a natural consequence of the multi-voiced nature of 'Sorry Song' and its dependence on constructing or appealing to a viable collectivity for its embodied 'we'. By harnessing the affective and embodied character of participatory music, 'Sorry Song' strives to forge a new kind of empathetic and mutually implicated Australian society.

4 Chanie's Story

At approximately the same time as Indigenous Australians were being subject to separation a system of mandatory residential schools for Aboriginal[40] people was established in Canada. These residential schools began in the 1880s and continued until the last school in Saskatchewan closed in 1996. As in Australia, the schools were intended to integrate Aboriginal children into European culture and religion through a policy of 'aggressive assimilation' that included the suppression of Indigenous languages and customs. Underfunded and with substandard academic and vocational programmes, the schools, which served 150,000 students over their history, were rife with physical, emotional, and sexual abuse. In 2008, the Canadian government and representatives of Indigenous peoples launched a Truth and Reconciliation Commission (hereafter TRC) to investigate the facts about the residential schools and to lay a foundation for national reconciliation. The Canadian TRC issued its final report, entitled *Honouring the Truth, Reconciling for the Future*, in December 2015. It is scathing in its assessment of the role of residential schools as a 'central element of [Canada's Aboriginal] policy which can best be described as "cultural genocide"' (TRC of Canada, 2015b, 1); yet, it also points out that uncovering this truth is only the first step towards reconciliation.

As in Australia, in the wake of this national reckoning with this history, music has emerged as a part of wider processes of reconciliation and remembrance. One of the key endeavours has been *Secret Path*, a multimedia project conceived by the white Canadian rock musician Gord Downie. The project has multiple artistic elements that have been combined in different configurations. The project originated with a set of poems written by Downie in 2013 and eventually turned into a ten-track solo music album by Downie, Kevin Drew (of Broken Social Scene), and Dave Hamelin (of The Stills). This is complemented by a graphic novel combining Downie's poems with illustrations by the white Canadian artist Jeff Lemire (who also provided the album artwork). In 2016, album (G. Downie, 2016) and novel (Downie and Lemire, 2016) were released together. At the premiere performance of *Secret Path* in Toronto in October of that year, Downie sang the album live, accompanied by an animated film version of Lemire's illustrations directed by Justin Stephenson. In addition, there is a short documentary directed and produced by Downie and his brother Mike that embeds the album and animated film within discussions of the inspiration for the project and the work of reconciliation in Canada more broadly (M. Downie, 2016). (See Figure 4 for a complete track listing from the music album.)

---

[40] In Canada, the term 'Aboriginal' encompasses all the peoples who lived in an area before the arrival of European explorers. It is an accepted umbrella term that covers three main groups of people in Canada: the First Nations, the Inuit, and the Métis. Indigenous is also an accepted term, but is used more often in an international context. I will use both 'Aboriginal' and 'Indigenous' in this section.

The Stranger (3'27")
Swing Set (9'03")
Seven Matches (12'27")
I Will Not Be Struck (16'15")
Son (20'30")
The Secret Path (23'57")
Don't Let This Touch You (28'15")
Haunt Them, Haunt Them, Haunt Them (33'27")
The Only Place to Be (38'44")
Here, Here and Here (41'48")

Figure 4 Track listing for *Secret Path*, with timings taken from documentary film *Gord Downie's The Secret Path* (https://secretpath.ca)

These different media converge in telling the story of Chanie (also known as Charlie) Wenjack. Wenjack was a member of the Marten Falls Ojibwe First Nation in northern Ontario who, at the age of nine, was sent to live at the Cecilia Jeffrey Indian Residential School in Kenora, Ontario. In October 1966, twelve-year-old Chanie, along with two other boys, Ralph and Jackie MacDonald, ran away from the school. They made it to the home of one of the MacDonalds' relatives about twenty miles from Kenora, where they stayed for a few days before Chanie determined to press on alone. Dressed in a light windbreaker and without money, maps, or other supplies save some matches, he set off to walk or catch a lift on a freight train home to Ogoki Post almost four hundred miles north. He made it a further twelve miles before perishing from starvation and exposure; his body was discovered next to the train tracks on 23 October 1966. A near-contemporary account of the boy's death by the journalist Ian Adams, published in the Canadian magazine *Maclean's* in February 1967, purports to capture something of the wider mood when it notes:

> It's not so unusual that Indian children run away from the residential schools they are sent to. They do it all the time, and they lose their toes and their fingers to frostbite. Sometimes they lose a leg or an arm trying to climb aboard freight trains. Occasionally, one of them dies. And perhaps because they are Indians, no one seems to care very much. (Adams, 1967, 30)

Adams's assessment of Canadian society's blasé attitudes towards Indigenous peoples notwithstanding, Chanie's death did result in the first inquest into the residential schools. It found that the residential school system caused 'tremendous emotional and adjustment problems' for children, but beyond suggesting that a study be made as to the rightness of the aims of Indigenous education, it stopped short of recommending change in the administration or aims of the system (TRC of Canada, 2015a, 349–50). The schools themselves were eventually phased out as day schools became more common on Indigenous reserves; between 1986 and 2009, the churches involved in running the residential schools offered apologies to residential school students for past abuses, and on 11 June 2008, shortly after the TRC was established, then-Prime Minister Stephen Harper delivered the federal government's official apology for the treatment Aboriginal children received in the schools.

Gord Downie himself was introduced to the story of Chanie Wenjack via his brother and bandmate Mike Downie, who initially came across the account in a radio documentary and then found and passed on Adams's 1967 article to his brother (Martin, 2016). However, Downie is far from the only artist to have engaged with Wenjack's story. Of artistic responses to Chanie's story produced around the time of the surge in reconciliatory activity occasioned by the TRC's Final Report, Heather Macfarlane (2018) lists music by the 'electric powwow' band A Tribe Called Red, a short animated film called 'SNIP' by Terril Calder, and various works by the writer Joseph Boyden; in the years since, numerous others have taken up the cause of telling the stories of those sent to residential schools.[41] Moreover, these were preceded by a few, mostly Aboriginal, artists who re-presented Wenjack's story in the 1970s, including the folk singer Willie Dunn and the writer Lee Maracle. Yet, as Macfarlane notes, these Indigenous storytellings never made much of an impact outside the Indigenous community. This lends credence to Downie's claim in the framing interview sections of the documentary *Gord Downie's The Secret Path* that 'down south none of us – I'm fifty-two – heard a darn thing about what was happening up here, at all'.[42] Yet, while Downie's ignorance of the residential school system active throughout his childhood might be explained in part by having grown up in Ontario, where the last residential school closed in 1973, the heritage of the residential schools was ever-present for Aboriginal communities. In other words, Downie's personal discovery of Wenjack is also a discovery for Canada's settler-colonist society of a story that has remained part of the living memory of many Aboriginal people. It is in part this divide between the experiences of Aboriginal and settler Canadians that *Secret Path* attempts to overcome.

Thus, according to Downie, *Secret Path*, which premiered in October 2016 on the fiftieth anniversary of Wenjack's death, 'acknowledges a dark part of

---

[41] NB: Calder (Métis) and the members of A Tribe Called Red (First Nations) are of Aboriginal heritage, while Boyden's claims to Aboriginal heritage have been controversial and, thus far, unsubstantiated. Among other efforts, Calder also has another short film focusing on Wenjack, called *Keewaydah (Let's Go Home)* and premiered on 21 October 2017.

[42] *Secret Path*, documentary film 50'00"–50'07", https://secretpath.ca (accessed 7 January 2020).

Canada's history [...] with the hope of starting our country on a road to reconciliation'.[43] In the past few years it has received substantial support from government organisations, including a special television broadcast of the animated film on 23 October 2016, and has generated further engagements with this story, including a documentary about the making of *Secret Path*, book clubs, and plays.[44] Other iterations of this public drive for reconciliation include the charitable Gord Downie & Chanie Wenjack Fund, which has received substantial funding from the Canadian government to 'continue the conversation that began with Chanie Wenjack's residential school story'; as of 2020, this includes supporting Legacy Spaces and Legacy Schools programmes, running Secret Path Week (an annual event commemorating the legacies of Downie and Wenjack), and promoting what the organisation calls 'reconciliACTIONs', or 'meaningful actions that move reconciliation forward'.[45] Recently, the songs have been used as the basis for elementary school lessons teaching literacy and Canadian history (Nyznik, 2017), and the animated film of Lemire's illustrations and Downie's music is available to all via the website https://secretpath.ca. In all this variety, *Secret Path* emerges as the initial impetus for a significant, multifaceted, transmedial storytelling that promotes the acknowledgment of the suffering of Canada's Indigenous peoples through broadcasting Wenjack's individual story.

The multiple formats of *Secret Path* makes assessing its repercussions for conflict transformation challenging. In this study, though, I focus on what I consider *Secret Path*'s most significant form: Downie's poetry transformed into song and presented together with Lemire's illustrations as a live performance and (in a slightly different version) in the animated film.[46]

The musical component of *Secret Path* comprises ten songs, each (with the exception of 'Son') sung in the first person by Downie as the character of Chanie Wenjack. The songs demonstrate a range of musical styles, from the driving rhythms and rock styling of 'Swing Set' to the soft, strained falsetto voice and acoustic guitar of 'Seven Matches' and the bass register piano ballad of 'Secret Path'. Throughout, Downie's sparse, sometimes cryptic lyrics suggest a series of attempts to illuminate facets of Chanie's interior life through asking (as he puts it in 'The Stranger') 'what is in my head? And what's in my chest?'

---

[43] Gord Downie, 'Statement', https://secretpath.ca (accessed 7 January 2020).

[44] See CBC news features available on https://gem.cbc.ca (not available outside of Canada); https://bit.ly/325758C (accessed 7 January 2020).

[45] CBC News (2018). See also The Gord Downie and Chanie Wenjack Fund, https://downiewenjack.ca/our-work (accessed 7 January 2020).

[46] A live version of 'Here, Here, and Here' from the October 2016 performance in Ottawa can be viewed on YouTube. Uploaded by a321doc, 21 October 2016, 5'29", www.youtube.com/watch?v=-2MRNmcPogo (accessed 7 January 2020). The animated film version is available on https://secretpath.ca, 41'48"–45'55".

In contrast to the relentless interior focus of the lyrics, Lemire's visual perspective is akin to that of an omniscient narrator, alternating between showing Chanie moving through the world and seeing it through Chanie's eyes. Drawn almost entirely in shades of blue and grey punctuated by shocks of black (hair, trees, the teachers' clothing, Chanie's pupils) and white (snow, light), the impression Lemire's depiction creates is of an interior and exterior landscape both dim and forbidding. This makes the occasional use of warm yellow-orange tones (the striking of the matches in 'Seven Matches' or the fire at the beginning of 'Son') all the more conspicuous. By far the most common use of these warm colours is when Chanie dreams of home and of his father, thereby sharpening the contrast between the cold surroundings of the residential school and the Canadian wilderness and the comfort of home and family.

Each of these remarkably compact songs crystallises some element of Chanie's life, but it is the final song 'Here, Here and Here' that offers a particularly intense moment of reckoning with his story (see Figure 5 for the lyrics). Sonically, it opens with hollow, buzzy, ringing synthesizer tones at once grimly mechanical and yet evocative of wind moving through the trees. Over a series of increasingly close-up visual shots of Chanie's prone figure intercut with black screens, the synthesizer indicates both a kind of emptiness and an approaching menace. This is undercut by

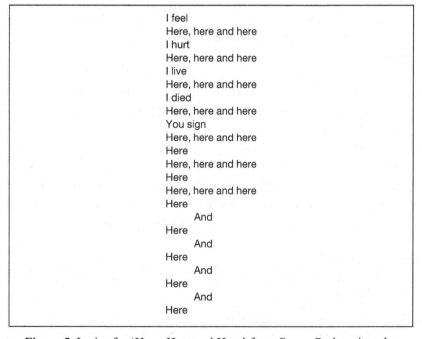

Figure 5 Lyrics for 'Here, Here and Here' from *Secret Path*, written by Gord Downie, used by permission.

the appearance of an arpeggiated figure in the bass register of the piano (quickly subject to large amounts of pitch bend) just as we see Chanie's face quiver and his eyes blink open slowly. As the piano part thickens and extends its melodic range, it comes to dominate the sonic texture, preparing the way for the voice. When Downie begins to sing in a rich middle register given additional reverb, he projects strongly over the instrumental texture as he navigates a disjunct melody punctuated with large pauses. This pattern of mellow piano arpeggiation and expansive vocal melody is established in the first lines and continues throughout.

Each repetition of the spare, six-note melody offers Downie the opportunity to inflect the text differently with slight changes in his vocal approach, and as the text moves through the increasing pathos of 'feel', 'hurt', 'live', and 'died', the sense of the lyrics as a litany grows. Initially, they conjure up the unspoken question: where does it hurt? We might imagine that the answer Downie sings begins in the body of a child indicating their wounds, but it swiftly takes on new layers until in the repetition of 'here, here and here' one can almost see a finger stabbing at a map, marking the locations of past and present pain. The 'I' who feels, hurts, lives, and dies in this song seems to be more than just Chanie; rather, it is a figure who encompasses the experience of Indigenous children and peoples all over Canada. Meanwhile, the transition after the fourth line to the second person, with its initially incongruous and faintly accusatory echo of signing a contract, also points in multiple directions: the treaties agreed (or not) between Indigenous and non-Indigenous peoples, the political policies establishing the residential schools, and perhaps even the official documents signed by grieving parents and communities receiving the bodies of children who perished at the schools.

The multiple associations of the lyrics are counterbalanced by Lemire's illustrations for the song (see Figure 6). From the initial view of Chanie huddled by the railroad tracks in the blowing snow, we see him struggle to rise, bending forward towards an otherworldly golden glow in front of him. This signals that Chanie has re-entered the dreamworld in which he imagines his home and family, and as he looks towards the dream-light, he sees his father gesturing for him in front of a house and bonfire. Just as Downie sings 'I died . . . here . . . here . . . and here', a wide-eyed Chanie pushes himself to his feet and moves hesitantly towards his father, eventually falling into his embrace. For a moment, it seems as though the song might end in this solace of the dreamworld, but as the piano rolls on, Chanie and his father look up and back to see Chanie's body still lying next to the railroad tracks. The visual image cuts away to show the boy's body in close-up, now with his eyes closed in death. As the golden light-filled spirit realm retreats over rolling piano figures and muffled drum hits, the visual perspective changes once again: now looking down at Chanie's body from above, the image recedes rapidly until it becomes evident that the audience is seeing though the

Figure 6 Video still from *Gord Downie's Secret Path in Concert.* Copyright Antica Productions, used by permission. Video available online.

pupil of a raven (a *manitou*, or guardian spirit) flying above the forest. (This is the same bird/spirit who promised to be with Chanie on 'that pale last day' in the previous song 'Haunt Them, Haunt Them, Haunt Them'.) As the landscape blurs, the sonic texture thins, but Downie's distorted voice remains just audible singing 'here and here and here and here and here'. These final words extend the poem's profound sense of double meaning: 'here, here, and here' are the numerous places and people for whom healing is necessary, but here too is a homonymic plea for the audience to 'hear' that need and to respond to it. Finally, the music, too, dwindles to the harsh caw of a raven, and we see an illustrated picture of Chanie that transforms into the photographic original: a young boy in a jacket and rubber boots, leaning against a door with a shy, happy smile on his face.

Given the absence of concrete documentation of the events leading into Chanie's death or knowledge of his emotions at the time, the choice to depict him in this way in 'Here, Here and Here' is an artistic licence for both poet-singer and illustrator; nonetheless, the differences between the expansion of the poetic subject and the focus of the artistic subject is striking. Both rely on pathos to create a sense of emotional attachment between the audience and the representation of Chanie. Lyrically, this is achieved through the consistent use of the first person and vivid sketches of the universal human experiences of loneliness, cold, and fear counter-balanced with a desire for home. Artistically, Lemire draws on well-established conventions connoting childhood in need of protection by depicting Chanie as wide-eyed, slight of figure, and frequently curled in self-protect-ively (over a desk, shrinking away from an authority figure, hunched over against the cold).[47] The slippage between the Chanie/first-person character whose emotional experiences are intimately familiar and the portrayal of a fragile child alone in an unfamiliar world is powerfully emotive.

This appeal to the pathetic is plausibly directed towards increasing the audience's feelings of empathy with Chanie by making his story familiar (that is, emphasising the ways in which his experience is like that of the audience) and relevant (that is, by re-presenting his story as deeply pertinent for the here and now). Nonetheless, it highlights the risk that the result may be one of paternalistic pity rather than of true empathy. This danger is ever-present wherever there is, borrowing Hannah Arendt's (1963) phrase, a 'spectacle of suffering' that separates the fortunate from the unfortunate without disturbing either the distance or the power relations that exist between them. Although it is possible for pity to motivate actions of redress, it remains an inadequate basis for reconfiguring social relations pursuant to transforming conflict. The transformation of Chanie's suffering in *Secret Path* into a cause for action is further complicated by Chanie's dual role as an individual who suffered in the past and a symbol for the wider suffering of Aboriginal peoples, which renders the perceived similarity on which empathy relies more difficult to attain. In the first of these roles, his lived experience is remote from that of the majority of *Secret Path*'s audience, while in the second, it is abstract. That is to say, even under a 'wide' definition of empathy – such as that proposed by de Waal (2008, 281) as a 'capacity to a) be affected by and share the emotional state of another b) assess the reasons for the other's state and c) identify with the other, adopting his or her perspective' – the ability for the contemporary audience of *Secret Path* to either share in Chanie's projected emotional state or to identify in a deep way with him seems limited.

If under the assumption that physical proximity is key for empathetic understanding we shift our attention to Downie as the apparent recipient of audience empathy, the ability of the audience to share in Downie's emotional state in his live performance of *Secret Path* likewise is circumscribed. Yet, he is nonetheless a key factor in increasing audience empathy with Chanie and with Aboriginal experience more broadly through the cultivation of a performing persona that mediates between what we might call 'settler Canada' and 'Aboriginal Canada'. Given the structure of *Secret Path* as channelling the audience's identification through the performing persona of Downie, the key question then becomes: how does *Secret Path* reconstitute the social relations in play? By re-presenting Chanie's inner and outer life in

---

[47] For more on the relationship between physical characteristics and emotional reactions, see Ngai (2012).

an emotionally effective manner, it closes the distance in felt experience between audience and Chanie even as the paratexts of its performance construct and advocate for a settler subject position that acknowledges moral responsibility. Taken as a whole, *Secret Path* thereby demonstrates ways of moving beyond empathy's experiential openness towards concrete social transformation.

This raises the further question of what kind of reconciliation or conflict transformation *Secret Path* might accomplish. In contrast to the enacted apology and embodied empathetic response of 'Sorry Song', I suggest that *Secret Path* has twin foci: first, raising the profile of Aboriginal peoples by broadcasting Chanie's experience (thereby establishing societal knowledge of the residential school system and Chanie as an individual and a symbol for its victims); and second, encouraging largely white settler-colonial audiences to adopt a subject position that acknowledges their implication in this history of abuse and their corresponding moral responsibility for it. Both of these aims are potentially available to a wide range of musical activities that engage either with Chanie's story or with the history of Aboriginal residential schools more generally. But *Secret Path*'s position within Canadian society, combined with Downie's own performing persona, place it in the centre of discussions over what it means to be Canadian in the wake of the revelations regarding the history of treatment of Aboriginal peoples.

While cross-cultural comparison has often been viewed with some suspicion, especially within anthropologically oriented music research, juxtaposing 'Sorry Song' and *Secret Path* clarifies different arrangements of the relationship between music, guilt, and conflict within two societies at analogous stages of conflict transformation. Despite their geographical distance, Australia and Canada share a history of white settler colonisation (largely stemming from the British Isles) wherein Indigenous populations have been marginalised and missionised in similar fashions. They remain societies in which the descendants of the colonisers retain political, social, and demographic dominance (Indigenous peoples make up 3 to 5 per cent of each country's population). Unlike other common locations for studying music and conflict such as Rwanda, the Balkans, South Africa, or Northern Ireland, the historical conflict with which each engages is not one of recent, violent armed conflict, neither is there a history of sectarian or political conflict; rather, both of these examples are marked as processes of reckoning with historical abuse and its contemporary resonances within liberal democracies. They thus illustrate some methods for musical conflict transformation that are particularly relevant within liberal democratic societies, but the patterns of musical engagement they demonstrate also point to wider possibilities.

However, although both of these case studies arise from similar social contexts and emotive histories, several factors mitigate equating either *Secret Path* as a whole or 'Here, Here and Here' with the Australian chorus of 'Sorry Song'. The first of these is the very different performance forms the two projects take. 'Sorry Song' exemplifies a broadly participatory music-making that resembles Turino's essentially communal model but also extends beyond that narrow definition to include the semi-spontaneous participation of audiences. *Secret Path*, despite its investment in creating community response, is far more akin to Turino's 'presentational' style in that the figure of Downie serves to channel the audience's responses to Chanie and to the conflict it attempts to reconcile.

Contributing to this distinction are differences in the roles of the composer and performer: while Fletcher largely composes for other performers and lacks widespread personal recognition in Australia, Downie, the lead singer and lyricist for the Canadian rock band The Tragically Hip, was one of Canada's best-known musical celebrities at the time he wrote *Secret Path*. In August 2016, he was even described by a Canadian journalist as 'the country's spirit animal in the only way a 52-year-old white man can legitimately be classified as a "spirit animal"' (Koentges, 2016). This link to a singular composer/performer in *Secret Path* was only strengthened by the timing of *Secret Path*'s release: two months after the close of Downie's concert tour with The Tragically Hip (the final concert of which was watched by roughly one in three Canadians), and less than six months after the singer announced that he had been diagnosed with terminal cancer.[48] The three performances in October 2016 that make up the premiere of *Secret Path* were themselves to become Downie's final full concert performances, and in critic Ben Rayner's (2016) words, 'the spectacle of Downie [...] constantly pacing back and forth in theatrical first-person facsimile of Wenjack's determined march towards oblivion whilst struggling publicly with terminal brain cancer only lent the heavier-than-heavy material more weight'. The close identification of *Secret Path* with Downie as an individual provides a strong and continuing connection between Chanie and Downie's personal trajectories that contrasts with the varying, non-exclusive sets of performers in 'Sorry Song'.

The expectations generated by musical genre are likewise key factors in distinguishing the two efforts. Although *Secret Path* was released under

---

[48] Downie announced his diagnosis via The Tragically Hip's website on 24 May 2016; despite his illness and fragile health, the band toured in the summer of 2016, with the final concert (viewed by an estimated 11.7 million people live and via broadcast/streaming by CBC) in Toronto on 20 August 2016. Downie's final album, the solo project *Introduce Yerself*, was released on 27 October 2017: ten days after his death from a glioblastoma.

Downie's own name rather than that of 'The Hip' (as the band are known to fans), Downie's musical style audibly draws on the conventions of indie- and progressive-rock music. For example, the range of instrumental sounds demands a relatively complex musical set-up covering both acoustic and electronic instruments, while the song melodies are adapted to suit Downie's particular vocal capabilities rather than the singalong style characteristic of 'Sorry Song' or other protest anthems. In fact, there is little to suggest that the songs on *Secret Path* were meant to be sung communally even in the context of a concert singalong; rather, they give the impression of objects for contemplation. Furthermore, the texts for *Secret Path*, which as I mentioned began as a series of poems written by Downie, are complex and allusive in their imagining of fragments of Wenjack's story told in a limited first-person voice. Without the additional context offered by Lemire's illustrations or external knowledge of Wenjack's story (or, given Downie's often muttered delivery, reading the accompanying lyrics to assist in their comprehension), many of the songs would be difficult to interpret. This is not necessarily unusual given conventions of singer-songwriter vocal style, and even though the songs' semantic content is less straightforwardly communicated than that of 'Sorry Song', this elusiveness does not preclude its affective power.

These factors warn against interpreting different reconciliatory efforts as strictly analogous, and a closer look reveals that *Secret Path* functions in a manner quite different than that of 'Sorry Song'. Rather than offering an opportunity for communal apology, *Secret Path* focuses on bringing the story of a single individual to a wider public. In *Secret Path*, Downie comes to embody a complex symbolic cluster encompassing Chanie's individual experience and the experiences both past and present of Aboriginal peoples, alongside a powerful, if often vague, sense of what it is to be Canadian. Moreover, by identifying himself alternately as Wenjack and as an individual complicit in perpetuating a discriminatory system, Downie offers a model for white settlers to identify with Indigenous people and recognise their own role in this difficult history. Through his performance, Downie turns Chanie Wenjack's story into a channel for publicly acknowledging the damaging effects of the residential school system. Downie also acknowledges moral responsibility on both personal and societal levels, moving smoothly from the individual to the collective and thereby offering a distinctive approach to music, guilt, and conflict transformation. Like 'Sorry Song', this mode of conflict transformation includes the empathetic identification with other, but here, this empathy is mediated by an individual performer who stands in as a symbol of both the empathised-with and the implicated subjects.

5 Reckoning with Sonic Histories

5.1 Assessing Performance Potential

In discussing 'Sorry Song' and *Secret Path*, I have focused on their potential for transforming conflict rather than attempting to appraise the extent to which they actually accomplish this transformation. Evaluating the success of any reconciliation effort is fraught with a multitude of difficulties, not least in defining what such success looks like in any particular setting: cessation of hostilities, self-reported changes in attitudes, altered voting patterns, legal restitution, and wider social changes are all potential markers. Yet even when positive trends in social reconciliation are detected, they are likely to be influenced by a number of different factors, making the disentangling of music's influence from that of other activities a significant problem. Evidence of change effected through music or performance has tended to rely on psychological studies and attitudinal data (as in the 'Resonant Community' project in Norway) or on anecdotal evidence collected from participants.[49] Both of these methods of assessment are illuminating, yet imperfect, with the latter method exposed to the charges of privileging transient experience or being open to undue influence on the part of those assessing the change. In particular, they do not clarify the grounds on which music might move participants from merely thinking better of 'others' (however they are constructed) to taking action to redress past wrongs.

I suggests that music's ability to encourage both empathy and the acknowledgement of moral responsibility is linked to the capacity of musical performance to model relationships between individuals or between social groups. This staging of morally implicated subject positions is significant for understanding music's role in identity formation and consequently, in conflict transformation. Whether we consider a work to be more participatory or presentational in its mode of performance, one key aspect of music's work in transforming conflict is its capacity to demonstrate and enact ways of being in the world – specifically, to model humanity's mutual implication. In other words, musical performance is peculiarly well-suited to the disclosure of what psychologist Kenneth Gergen (2009) calls our 'relational being'.[50] Although the spectre of substituting emotional catharsis for action is never far off when it comes to music and conflict, musical performances that promote empathy

---

[49] For more on 'Resonant Community' see Skyllstad (1995, 2000). Thirteen years after 'Resonant Community' ended, Arild Bergh (2007) followed up with participants and discovered little lasting impact on participants' everyday lives, raising questions about the how effective musical interventions are in the long term.

[50] I'm grateful to Nicholas Cook for introducing me to Gergen's evocative phrase.

alongside acceptance of moral responsibility offer one possibility for increasing senses of relationality and facilitating genuine social change.

Due to the nature of the conflicts with which they engage, the relational characters of both 'Sorry Song' and *Secret Path* are diffuse. In engaging with a performance of either work the audience is confronted by both an abstract entity – in the form of communal history – and a disturbingly present, yet foreign, 'other' in the shape of another's lived experience. This conflict is evident in the linguistic structures of 'Sorry Song', which give voice to the tensions between the variously constructed 'us' and 'them' factions that face Australia and all multicultural societies. Fletcher first establishes this classification of difference as essential for the act of apologising before encouraging her audience of both singers and listeners to move beyond that identity binary with the recognition that 'we' must include members of different ethnic and social groups. Moreover, participants in 'Sorry Song' performances are asked to enact an empathetic identification with others, whether by corporal action such as standing in respect or joining hands, or through musical harmony. In place of a plethora of evocative first-person vocal fragments, Fletcher offers a unified narrative of reconciliation that encourages non-Indigenous Australians to identify themselves first with a difficult past and then with the Indigenous Australians who continue to suffer from history's wrongs. In the case of *Secret Path*, the narrative is less obviously one of unity or reconciliation; rather, it presents a singular story as call for acknowledgement, repentance, and action. By reanimating Chanie as an individual, Downie and Lemire convert his story into widespread public knowledge even as they suggest further avenues for communal response. In particular, *Secret Path* has served as the catalyst for extensive community reconciliation work that extends beyond the capacity of a single multimedia project.

Both of these pieces thus have the potential to contribute to acknowledging the past, encouraging identification between different groups, and increasing empathic responses through offering spaces for implication and reconciliation. In doing so, they must navigate a delicate line between encouraging openness and provoking a backlash that works against the production of empathy. One of the issues facing societies dealing with historical violence and discrimination is the disruption such revelations have on the majority community's sense of identity. Downie confronts key identity processes in the statement accompanying *Secret Path* in which he claims, 'This is about Canada. [...] Canada is not Canada. We are not the country we think we are.'[51] The consequences of Downie's demand to broaden the understanding of what Canada is and has been were particularly pungent in 2016 when Canada was wrestling with the

---

[51] Downie, 'Statement', https://secretpath.ca (accessed 7 January 2020).

magnitude of the TRC's findings even as it celebrated the sesquicentennial anniversary of the Canadian Confederation (with its attendant patriotic displays celebrating what it means to be Canadian), yet his statement is not as clear as it may seem on first sight. On the one hand, it is a straightforward claim about ideals of national identity and behaviour, though one lent extra weight by coming from a man considered by many (at least of a certain age and linguistic-cultural heritage) to embody Canadian identity. On the other hand, there is an elision in both Downie's statement and much of the discourse surrounding him between Downie as a nationalist and Downie as an Indigenous rights activist, in other words, between settler Canada and Indigenous Canada. As Macfarlane (2018) notes, this reveals an underlying assumption that Canadian national identity stems from the former and can be extended to encompass the latter. In this way, to be Canadian (even one invested in the reconciliation process) replicates the very logic of settlement that gave rise to the residential school system.

Similar questions of historical responsibility and the negotiation of postcolonial identity have been salient in Australia's public debates over the legacy of the Stolen Generations. For her part, Fletcher avoids suggestions of culpability, preferring to focus on questions of truth, as in an interview with the ethnomusicologist Katelyn Barney where she claims: 'we certainly hope this song helps to change the truth of my generation so there's no chance that these kids won't know what happened here' (Barney, 2012, 79). In this way, every performance of 'Sorry Song' contributes to the acknowledgement of the past by increasing the visibility of the Stolen Generations and reinforcing the truth of their experiences. Through this slow process of proclaiming truth and transforming knowledge of history into widespread acknowledgement of its past injustice and present implications, society itself may be transformed.

In addition to disrupting historical senses of identity, both of these works raise questions about the continuing impact of race on the arts, in that the prominence of these white composers threatens to perpetuate the erasure of Indigenous voices. In this, Fletcher has an advantage in that she does not have to contend with the dynamics of celebrity or the prominence that comes with being a solo performer; as a long-standing activist who works closely with Indigenous peoples, she is perhaps less vulnerable to charges of appropriation than other white settler composers. Moreover, as an enacted gesture of apology, it seems fitting that 'Sorry Song' would be written by a white settler composer. Though some might argue that victims' voices should be more prominent within the song itself, this might be countered by noting that Indigenous musicians – whether Madjitil Moorna or others – have played a prominent role in its performance. Evaluating Downie's work in *Secret Path* is somewhat more complex as neither he nor any of the other participants in the project are of

Indigenous heritage, despite the fact that he adopts an Indigenous story and voice in his work. Macfarlane (2018) criticises Downie for his lack of acknowledgement of the parallel life of Chanie's story within the Indigenous community, and especially for what she insists is his appropriation of the boy's voice through his first-person embodiment. Yet Downie went to remarkable lengths to include the surviving members of Chanie's family in *Secret Path*, for example by welcoming more than thirty members of the Wenjack family onstage at the project's 2016 live premiere and including footage of a visit to their remote hometown of Ogoki Post, Ontario, in the documentary film. The charitable organisation that grew from the project, the Gord Downie & Chanie Wenjack Fund, is Indigenous-led and includes on its board of directors representatives of both families (in 2020, Mike Downie and Harriet Visitor, respectively) alongside other members from different Aboriginal groups. These gestures of acceptance and inclusion were returned when, shortly after the premiere of *Secret Path*, the chiefs of the Assembly of First Nations gifted Downie with a Lakota spirit name at an eagle feather ceremony in recognition of his work in advancing Indigenous causes. The singer's prominence was highlighted further in June 2017 when he received the Order of Canada given for Outstanding Indigenous Leadership. Nonetheless, it is a challenge to extricate the project of *Secret Path* from Downie's own performing persona and personal narrative of illness and death. Despite the fact that in the last few years of his life he actively used his celebrity to highlight Indigenous causes, in evaluating the media coverage lavished on Downie it is difficult to avoid the feeling that the expressions of the famous white person are being substituted for the voices and understanding of Indigenous peoples. Going forward, continuing to centre Chanie's story and connecting it to both the lived experiences of other Indigenous individuals and to wider human experiences will be key to bringing greater acknowledgement of white Canadian implication in this history.

5.2 Legacies of Performance

In looking beyond the immediate impact of these performances on their audiences to the wider state of conflict transformation in their respective countries, the picture of reconciliation becomes muddier. In Australia, the euphoria demonstrated in the 2008 Madjitil Moorna performance has been only sporadically recaptured. In some ways, despite the National Apology, the government has continued the 'practical reconciliation' policy enacted under the mid-1990s Howard government, which prioritised addressing socio-economic disadvantage over broader issues of justice or symbolic acts of reconciliation. In particular, the National Apology itself came hard on the heels of the establishment of the Northern Territory Emergency Response (NTER), an initiative aimed at tackling social woes amongst the Indigenous population in which various commentators have identified echoes of the language of the very child removal policies for which the Apology asked forgiveness (Pilger, 2014; Young, 2014).[52] The decade since the Apology has also seen a wider collapse of progressive public discourse and rise of anti-apology movements in Australia and elsewhere, diminishing confidence in Elazar Barkan's (2000) announcement of the advent of a 'new international morality'.[53] As of 2020, the NTER's successor (2012's *Stronger Futures in the Northern Territory Act*) remains controversially in place and the legacy of discrimination so hopefully absent in 'Sorry Song' continues to have an impact on Australian society.

Although Canada's post-TRC reconciliation process is still relatively young, Aboriginal communities, many of whom remain isolated and under-resourced, are alert to signs of a prematurely slowing engagement with reconciliatory processes of social change. It is telling that when Chanie's sister Pearl Achneepineskum commented in 2016 on what benefit she wished to see accrue to the Indigenous community she highlighted the continuing need for secondary schools to be built on every reserve so that children do not have to be sent away from their families for schooling.[54] Preventing Aboriginal children from experiencing the same kind of dislocation and isolation as Chanie did would be a fitting culmination to this retelling of his story, but that the lack of educational provision remains an issue is also an indictment of the slow progress.

There are a multitude of challenges facing conflict transformation processes in Canada and Australia, the solutions to many of which seem far beyond the capacity of music to address. Despite the intuitive desire to affirm, in Cervantes' words, that 'he who sings scares away his woes', cycles of poverty, deprivation, and disease cannot be broken by song.[55] Neither can the systemic racial discrimination that has sustained those cycles. Yet the musical combination of acknowledgement and apology has the potential to reshape what it means to be either Australian or Canadian today and thus contribute to transforming these conflicts.

---

[52] Both the NTER and the current 'Stronger Futures' policy have come under heavy criticism as racially and culturally discriminatory by organisations such as Amnesty International.

[53] For one pre-Apology perspective on the situation in Australia that nonetheless highlights some of the issues that have become salient since 2008, see Augoustinos and LeCouteur (2004).

[54] Pearl Achneepineskum, 'and you know what I want from this? Is that I want high schools, schools, to be built on every reserve [...] so children don't have to leave', *Secret Path* (documentary film), 52'40"–52'56", https://secretpath.ca (accessed 7 January 2020).

[55] The context here is Don Quixote's encounter with a man who was sentenced to the galleys after 'singing under suffering' – i.e. confessing under torture. Miguel de Cervantes, *Don Quixote de la Mancha*, pt. 1, ch. 22. https://bit.ly/3jgWONJ (accessed 20 August 2020).

6 How Music Can Help

Lurking behind any project that positions music as potentially transformative of conflict is a question – not of music's function (as I have already suggested, the specific meanings and functions of music as a general phenomenon are too manifold to be neatly enumerated), but of music's relationship to the contradictions inherent in the society which it seeks to influence. How does a given performance or work sustain, undermine, reflect, or hide those contradictions? To what degree is the music as a phenomenon implicated in the very structures of conflict it seeks to overturn?

There are some who might argue that pieces like 'Sorry Song' and *Secret Path* are simply too marginal (or even banal) to give effective perspectives on musical conflict transformation. Surely there are better compositions out there – or if not, surely there are other aspects of music that would provide a more incisive commentary? In fact, I have made no claims here that either of these works exhibits the kind of quality associated with acclaim in Western art music, but this is not because I believe them to be masterworks, but because the question of quality is irrelevant in this context. To offer a rather facetious rejoinder to that question, if it were discovered that the 'I Love You' song from the children's television show *Barney the Dinosaur* brought peace to the world we would find ourselves singing it on loop. It is true, that – like almost all music that has ever existed – these pieces will eventually be lost from the performed repertoire, but that does not mean that they will have had no impact. In fact, it would almost seem to be the goal of musical conflict transformation to play itself out. The alternative wherein musical pieces such as these were perpetually in demand would suggest a state of permanent potential for conflict, incapable of meaningful change.

Given that both of these pieces have as their *raison d'être* the possibility of transforming conflicts in their respective societies, the forthrightness with which each of their creators has promoted the music as a means of generating some form of reconciliation should lead us to take the issue of music's efficacy seriously. There is ample room in the journalistic reception of these pieces for the heightened rhetoric common to descriptions of musical reconciliation efforts, yet (notably in the case of *Secret Path*) the sense is that of musical performance as a sobering call to action: '[the album's] ambition is heavy; its cause significant' (Wheeler, 2016). Instead of a heady rush to emotional catharsis, what each of these works suggests is that music offers a means for audiences and performers to enact memory, apology, or reconciliation in ways that shape their relationships with themselves, others, and society.

One of the striking features of the continuing lives of both *Secret Path* and 'Sorry Song' is their adoption as accessories to the educational curriculum in their respective countries. Whether as a tool for teaching a difficult part of history and of general consciousness-raising, or as a concrete means for both performers and audiences to act out apology and reconciliation across the country, *Secret Path* and 'Sorry Song' fulfil distinct social and musical functions tied to the widespread belief in music's power to persuade and transform society on both an individual and a collective level. Understandably, they differ in the kinds of truth, acknowledgement, and reconciliation they offer. This is in part due to the contrasting kinds of musical participation they encourage. In the case of 'Sorry Song', it is notable that it is almost wholly performed and has a very limited 'archival' existence in Taylor's (2003) sense of the term; since Downie's death it seems clear that the continuing impact of the music-plus-visual form of *Secret Path* is dependent on its archival existence. Fletcher's and Downie's compositions thus exemplify two different, yet complementary, approaches to reconciliatory music. 'Sorry Song' provides opportunities for communities to enact apologies in a personally meaningful way, while *Secret Path* encourages widespread acknowledgement of the past and mobilises individual stories as a way of generating empathy and identification. Both pieces participate in creating a favourable climate for both private and public acts of contrition on individual and group levels. Taken together, they suggest that acknowledging the past while walking into the future can bring to light potential for shared understanding that might otherwise be hidden.

Thinking about the music's connections to both empathy and moral responsibility offers several advantages to those interested in untangling the relationship between music and conflict: it enhances our interpretation of what music might ideally be capable of while also helping us understand why many efforts seem to have little lasting effect; it provides a counterbalance to contemporary questions of identity by focusing attention on questions of agency and responsibility; and it better reflects a common need amongst those who have experienced conflict for their experiences to be not only recognised as factually true but also acknowledged within the public cognitive scene. By reflecting critically on the relationships between music, conflict, and guilt in a holistic fashion that encompasses the abstract through the musico-structural to the lived experience of participants, we can gain a better understanding of what the ideal of musical conflict transformation really entails.

* * *

The question 'how can music help?' posed at the beginning of this book sets off another series of questions: help with what? According to whom? What does 'can' signify in this context? Research from psychology to therapy to neurobiology suggests that in terms of producing positive emotions and feelings of solidarity the answer to the original question is a qualified yes, and points to empirical demonstrations of particular forms of musical participation as increasing empathetic responses to social outgroups. Yet, as I have shown, an ethical narrative that places its highest value on openness and empathy falls short of the rich potential afforded by music. The features of music that grant it a capacity to shape human experience and our approach to ourselves and others have the potential to act powerfully in the world, but this is a potential that remains tremendously difficult to harness for specific ends. If musical perform-ance is to be part of a meaningful 'integration of aesthetics and ethics' (Frith, 1996, 275) or to encourage the transformation of conflict, it requires us to think carefully about how music, empathy, and moral responsibility may intersect.

In his introduction to Primo Levi's *Moments of Reprieve*, Michael Ignatieff (2002, 3) declares that 'all of us have grown up in the moral shadow of the Holocaust' and for many – especially Western – readers that is certainly true. But as I write this in the summer of 2020 it is imperative to recognise that many of us have also grown up in other moral shadows, most of all that of white supremacy and the long and violent legacy of chattel slavery. These have too long been unacknowledged, and although I cannot claim here to have grasped all of the ways in which these have shaped my own scholarship and the discipline of music studies as a whole, they lie heavy across this work. Indeed, not to see this would be itself a failure of both empathy and moral responsibility. It was the assumption of white supremacy that drove the establishment of residential schools in Canada and the removal of Indigenous children from their families in Australia just as it was white supremacy that drove (and continues to drive) violence against Black, Indigenous, and people of colour in the United States of America and elsewhere. I know this, but as I have argued here, knowledge is a necessary but not sufficient condition for transformative change.

Given this, what is music, and more precisely, the musicians and scholars and audiences who engage in music, to do in the face of such knowledge? It is not only Fletcher and Downie, but also their collaborators and performers, their audiences and all who wrestle with the role of the arts in society who have to confront this question. There is no single answer any more than there is a single type of music potentially capable of transforming conflict, but the musical responses I examine here share core characteristics of empathetic listening to stories previously unheard or ignored, the intentional bringing forward of those experiences within the public communal sphere, and the dual recognition of moral responsibility for past wrongs and implication in present injustice. They affirm that music, in all its local manifestations and variety, has a special potential to offer a means of acknowledgement and acceptance as it incorpor-ates the past into the present. Most of all, there is an encouragement to act on that knowledge, to make a start on something new. 'Sorry Song' and *Secret Path* are but two examples of how music may work to produce new understanding and new actions of redress – in short, new audiences. Producing these new audiences (or rather, listener-performer-participants) means examining not only what it is to be Australian or to be Canadian – Indigenous and immigrant – but what it is to be human and to be at once empathetically moved by and morally implicated in the suffering of others.

References

Adams, I. (1967). The Lonely Death of Chanie Wenjack. *Maclean's*, February 1967, 30–1, 38–49, 42–3. www.macleans.ca/society/the-lonely-death-of-chanie-wenjack/ (accessed 7 January 2020).

Ahmed, S. (2004). *The Cultural Politics of Emotion*. Edinburgh: Edinburgh University Press.

Ansdell, G. (2014). *How Music Helps in Music Therapy and in Everyday Life*. Farnham: Ashgate.

Araujó, S. (2006). Conflict and Violence as Theoretical Tools in Present-Day Ethnomusicology: Notes on a Dialogic Ethnography of Sound Practices in Rio de Janeiro. *Ethnomusicology*, **50**(2), 287–313.

Arendt, H. (1958). *The Human Condition*. Chicago, IL: The University of Chicago Press.

Arendt, H. (1963). *On Revolution*. New York: Viking.

Augoustinos, M., and LeCouteur, A. (2004). On Whether to Apologize to Indigenous Australians: The Denial of White Guilt. In N. R. Branscombe and B. Doosje, eds., *Collective Guilt: International Perspectives*. Cambridge: Cambridge University Press, pp. 236–61.

Baker, G. (2018). El Sistema, 'The Venezuelan Musical Miracle': The Construction of a Global Myth. *Latin American Musical Review*, **39**(2), 160–93.

Barkan, E. (2000). *The Guilt of Nations*. New York: Norton.

Barney, K. (2012). Sing Loud, Break Through the Silence. *Perfect Beat*, **13**(1), 69–94.

Baron-Cohen, S. (2011). *Zero Degrees of Empathy: A New Theory of Human Cruelty*. London: Allen Lane.

Barrow, L. G. (2011). Guilt by Association: The Effect of Attitudes towards Fascism in the Critical Assessment of the Music of Ottorino Respighi. *International Review of the Aesthetics and Sociology of Music*, **42**(1), 79–95.

Bateson, G. (1972). *Steps to an Ecology of Mind*. London: Intertext Books.

Beckles Willson, R. (2009). The Parallax Worlds of the West–Eastern Divan Orchestra. *Journal of the Royal Musical Association*, **134**(2), 319–47.

Beckles Willson, R. (2013). *Orientalism and Musical Mission: Palestine and the West*. Cambridge: Cambridge University Press.

Behrendt, H., and Ben-Ari, R. (2012). The Positive Side of Negative Emotions: The Role of Guilt and Shame in Coping with Interpersonal Conflict. *Journal of Conflict Resolution*, **56**(6), 1116–38.

Benedict, R. (1946). *The Chrysanthemum and the Sword: Patterns of Japanese Culture*. Boston, MA: Houghton Mifflin.

Bergh A., and Sloboda, J. A. (2010). Music and Art in Conflict Transformation: A Review. *Music and Arts in Action*, **2**(2), 3–17.

Bergh, A. (2007). I'd Like to Teach the World to Sing: Music and Conflict Transformation. *Musica Scientiae,* Special Issue, 141–57.

Bergh, A. (2011). Emotions in Motion: Transforming Conflict and Music. In I. Deliège and J. W. Davidson, eds., *Music and the Mind: Essays in Honour of John Sloboda*. New York: Oxford University Press, pp. 363–78.

Branscombe, N. R., and Doosje, B., eds. (2004). *Collective Guilt: International Perspectives*. Cambridge: Cambridge University Press.

Brinner, B. (2009). *Playing Across a Divide*. Oxford: Oxford University Press.

Bronfman, A. (2016). *Isles of Noise: Sonic Media in the Caribbean*. Chapel Hill, NC: University of North Carolina Press.

Butler, J. (2004). *Precarious Life: The Powers of Mourning and Violence*. London: Verso.

Butler, J. (2010). *Frames of War: When is Life Grievable?* London: Verso.

CBC News. (2018). Downie-Wenjack Fund Received $5M in 2018 Federal Budget. 27 February 2018. https://bit.ly/318MFvZ (accessed 7 January 2020).

Clark, R. S. (2011). History of Efforts to Codify Crimes Against Humanity. In L. N. Sadat, ed., *Forging a Convention for Crimes Against Humanity*. Cambridge: Cambridge University Press, pp. 8–27.

Clarke, E. (2019). Empathy and the Ecology of Musical Consciousness. In R. Herbert, D. Clarke, and E. Clarke, eds., *Music and Consciousness 2: Worlds, Practices, Modalities*. New York: Oxford University Press, pp. 71–92.

Clarke, E., DeNora, T., and Vuoskoski, J. (2015a). Music, Empathy, and Cultural Understanding: Final Report. Arts and Humanities Research Council. https://bit.ly/2Q8S6oE

Clarke, E., DeNora, T., and Vuoskoski, J. (2015b). Music, Empathy, and Cultural Understanding. *Physics of Life Reviews*, **15**, 61–88.

Clough, P. ed. (2007). *The Affective Turn: Theorizing the Social*. Durham, NC: Duke University Press.

Coghlan, A. (2014). Prom 46 – Review. *The Independent*. 21 August. https://bit.ly/3h6KoqO (accessed 7 January 2020).

Connerton, P. (2012). *The Spirit of Mourning: History, Memory and the Body*. Cambridge: Cambridge University Press.

Cook, N. (1998). *Music: A Very Short Introduction*. Oxford: Oxford University Press.

Cook, N. (2013). *Beyond the Score*. New York: Oxford University Press.

Corn, A. (2011). Treaty Now: Popular Music and the Indigenous Struggle for Justice in Contemporary Australia. In I. Peddie, ed., *Popular Music and Human Rights, Volume II: World Music*. Farnham: Ashgate, pp. 17–26.

Cross, I. (1999). Is Music the Most Important Thing We Ever Did? Music, Development, and Evolution. In S. W. Yi, ed., *Music, Mind and Science*. Seoul: Seoul University Press, pp. 10–39.

Cross, I. (2012). Music as a Social and Cognitive Process. In P. Rebuschat et al., eds., *Language and Music as Cognitive Systems*. Oxford: Oxford University Press, pp. 315–28.

Cusick, S. G. (2006). Music as Torture/Music as Weapon. *TRANS: Revista Transcultural de Música*, **10**, n.p.

Danewid, I. (2017). White Innocence in the Black Mediterranean: Hospitality and the Erasure of History. *Third World Quarterly*, **38**(7), 1674–89.

de Waal, F. (2008). Putting the Altruism Back Into Altruism: The Evolution of Empathy. *Annual Review of Psychology*, **59**(1), 279–300.

de Waal, F. (2009). *The Age of Empathy: Nature's Lessons for a Kinder Society*. New York: Three Rivers Press.

DeNora, T. (1999). Music as Technology of the Self. *Poetics*, **27**, 31–56.

Deutsch, F., and Madle, R. A. (1975). Empathy: Historic and Current Conceptualizations, Measurement, and a Cognitive Theoretical Perspective. *Human Development*, **18**(4), 267–87.

Dieckmann, S., and Davidson, J. W., eds. (2019). Peace, Empathy and Conciliation through Music. *International Journal of Community Music*, Special Issue, 12(3), 293–400.

Downie, G. (2016). *Secret Path: For Chanie Wenjack*. CD. Wiener Art. Arts & Crafts Productions.

Downie, G., and Lemire, J. (2016). *Secret Path*. New York: Simon & Schuster.

Downie, M., dir. (2016). *The Secret Path*. eOne Television and the Canadian Broadcasting Company. https://secretpath.ca

Empathy for Peace. (2019). Empathy: An Invaluable Natural Resource for Peace. White Paper, September 2019. https://bit.ly/323ac0I (accessed 7 January 2020).

Fanon, F. (1965). This is the Voice of Algeria. In *A Dying Colonialism*, translated by Haakon Chevalier. New York: Grove Press, pp. 69–98.

Frith, S. (1996). *Performing Rites: On the Value of Popular Music*. Oxford: Oxford University Press.

Galtung, J. (2001). After Violence: Reconciliation, Reconstruction, and Resolution. In M. Abu-Nimer, ed., *Reconciliation, Justice and Coexistence*. Lanham, MD: Lexington Books, pp. 3–23.

Gergen, K. J. (2009). *Relational Being: Beyond Self and Community*. New York: Oxford University.

Gordy, E. (2013). *Guilt, Responsibility and Denial: The Past at Stake in Post-Milosevic Serbia*. Philadelphia, PA: University of Pennsylvania Press.

Grant, M. J., Möllemann, R., Morlandstö, I., Münz, S. C., and Nuxoll, C. (2010). Music and Conflict: Interdisciplinary Perspectives. *Interdisciplinary Science Reviews*, **35**(2), 183–98.

Gray, A.-M. (2008). Music as a Tool of Reconciliation in South Africa. In O. Urbain, ed., *Music and Conflict Transformation: Harmonies and Dissonances in Geopolitics*. London: I.B. Tauris & Co., pp. 63–77.

Gregg, M., and Siegworth, G., eds. (2010). *The Affect Theory Reader*. Durham, NC: Duke University Press.

Greitemeyer, T. (2009). Effects of Songs with Prosocial Lyrics on Prosocial Thoughts, Affect, and Behaviour. *Journal of Experimental Social Psychology*, **45**(1), 186–90.

Hall, G. (2015). West–Eastern Divan Orchestra. *The Guardian*. 19 August. https://bit.ly/3l2Unjw (accessed 7 January 2020).

Hall, P., ed. (2018). *The Oxford Handbook of Music Censorship*. New York: Oxford University Press.

Harrison, K., Mackinlay, E., and Pettan, S., eds. (2010). *Applied Ethnomusicology: Historical and Contemporary Approaches*. Newcastle-upon-Tyne: Cambridge Scholars Publishing.

Hartman, S. V. (1997). *Scenes of Subjection: Terror, Slavery and Self-Making in Nineteenth-Century America*. New York: Oxford University Press.

Haskell, E. (2015). The Role of Applied Ethnomusicology in Post-Conflict and Post-Catastrophe Communities. In S. Pettan and J. T. Titon, eds., *The Oxford Handbook of Applied Ethnomusicology*. New York: Oxford University Press, pp. 197–225.

Herndon, M. (2000). Epilogue. In P. Moisala and B. Diamond, eds., *Music and Gender*. Urbana, IL: University of Illinois Press, pp. 347–59.

Hirsch, A. K., ed. (2012). *Theorizing Post-Conflict Reconciliation: Agonism, Restitution and Repair*. London: Routledge.

Hoffman, M. (2000). *Empathy and Moral Development: Implications for Caring and Justice*. Cambridge: Cambridge University Press.

HREOC [Human Rights and Equal Opportunity Commission]. (1997). *Bringing Them Home: Report of the National Inquiry into the Separation of Aboriginal and Torres Strait Islander Children from Their Families*. https://bit.ly/2EiQg1w (accessed 7 January 2020).

HREOC [Human Rights and Equal Opportunity Commission]. (2002). *Bringing Them Home: Community Guide*. PDF archived at https://bit.ly/32a302Q (accessed 7 January 2020).

ICTM [International Council for Traditional Music]. (2007). *ICTM Study Group on Applied Ethnomusicology.* http://ictmusic.org/group/applied-ethnomusicology (accessed 1 July 2020).

Ignatieff, M. (2002). Introduction. In P. Levi, *Moments of Reprieve*, translated by Ruth Feldman. London: Penguin, pp. 3–7.

Johnson, B., and Cloonan, M. (2008). *Dark Side of the Tune: Popular Music and Violence.* Aldershot: Ashgate.

Jones, M. R., and Boltz, M. (1989). Dynamic Attending and Responses to Time. *Psychological Review,* **96**(3), 459–91.

Keil, C., and Feld, S. (1984). *Music Grooves.* Chicago, IL: University of Chicago Press.

Kivy, P. (2009a). Empty Pleasure to the Ear. In *Antithetical Arts: On the Ancient Quarrel between Literature and Music.* Oxford: Oxford University Press, pp. 235–62.

Kivy, P. (2009b). Musical Morality. In *Antithetical Arts: On the Ancient Quarrel between Literature and Music.* Oxford: Oxford University Press, pp. 216–34.

Koch, G., and Crowe, A. (2013). Song, Land, and Ceremony: Interpreting the Place of Songs as Evidence for Australian Aboriginal and Torres Strait Islander Land Claims. *Collaborative Anthropologies,* **6**, 373–98.

Koentges, C. (2016). The Lonely End of the Rink. *Slate.* 17 August. https://bit.ly/2Q3Gp2o (accessed 7 January 2020).

Krueger, J. (2019). Music as Affective Scaffolding. In R. Herbert, D. Clarke, and E. Clarke, eds., *Music and Consciousness 2: Worlds, Practices, Modalities.* New York: Oxford University Press, pp. 55–70.

Laurence, F. (2008). Music and Empathy. In O. Urbain, ed., *Music and Conflict Transformation: Harmonies and Dissonances in Geopolitics.* London: I.B. Tauris & Co., pp. 13–25.

Lederach, J. P. (2003). *The Little Book of Conflict Transformation.* Intercourse, PA: Good Books.

Levinas, E. (1969). *Totality and Infinity: An Essay on Exteriority.* Translated by Alphonso Lingis. Pittsburgh, PA: Duquesne University Press.

Levinson, J. (2015a). Popular Music as Moral Microcosm: Life Lessons from Jazz Standards. In *Musical Concerns: Essays in Philosophy of Music.* New York: Oxford University Press, pp. 115–30.

Levinson, J. (2015b). Shame in General and Shame in Music. In *Musical Concerns: Essays in Philosophy of Music.* New York: Oxford University Press, pp. 88–98.

Leys, R. (2007). *From Guilt to Shame: Auschwitz and After.* Princeton, NJ: Princeton University Press.

Lickel, B., Schmader, T., and Barquissau, M. (2004). The Evocation of Moral Emotions in Intergroup Contexts: The Distinction between Collective Guilt and Collective Shame. In N. R. Branscombe and B. Doosje, eds., *Collective Guilt: International Perspectives*. Cambridge: Cambridge University Press, pp. 35–55.

Lu, C. (2008). Shame, Guilt, and Reconciliation After War. *European Journal of Social Theory*, **11**(3), 367–83.

Macfarlane, H. (2018). The Resurrection of 'Charlie' Wenjack. *Canadian Literature* **236**, 92–110, 182.

Margalit, A. (2002). *The Ethics of Memory*. Cambridge, MA: Harvard University Press.

Martin, D. (2016). The Secret Path. Interview with Mike Downie. *CTV Television*. 18 October.

Martin, K. (2013). *Modernism and the Rhythms of Sympathy: Vernon Lee, Virginia Woolf, D.H Lawrence*. Oxford: Oxford University Press.

McCann, M. (1995). Music and Politics in Ireland: the Specificity of the Folk Revival in Belfast. *British Journal of Ethnomusicology*, **4**, 51–75.

McCoy, J. (2009). Making Violence Ordinary: Radio, Music, and the Rwandan Genocide. *African Music*, **8**(3), 85–96.

McGarty, C., and Bliuc, A.-M. (2004). Refining the Meaning of the 'Collective' in Collective Guilt: Harm, Guilt, and Apology in Australia. In N. R. Branscombe and B. Doosje, eds., *Collective Guilt: International Perspectives*. Cambridge: Cambridge University Press, pp. 112–29.

McMurray, P. 2019. Witnessing Race in the New Digital Cinema. In N. Cook, M. Ingalls, and D. Trippett, eds., *The Cambridge Companion to Music in Digital Culture*. Cambridge: Cambridge University Press, pp. 124–46.

Ngai, S. (2012). *Our Aesthetic Categories: Zany, Cute, Interesting*. Cambridge, MA: Harvard University Press.

Nyznik, J. (2017). Teacher's Lesson Plan Goes National. *Peterborough Examiner*, 1 November, A3.

Obama, B. (2006). Commencement Address. Northwestern University. 19 June. www.northwestern.edu/newscenter/stories/2006/06/barack.html (accessed 7 January 2020).

Obama, M. (2020). Speech. Democratic National Convention. 17 August. https://wapo.st/2E6Z4rT (accessed 20 August 2020).

O'Connell, J. M. (2010). Introduction. In J. M. O'Connell and S. Castelo-Branco, eds., *Music and Conflict*. Urbana, IL: University of Illinois Press, pp. 1–14.

Oxley, J. C. (2011). *The Moral Dimensions of Empathy: Limits and Applications in Ethical Theory and Practice*. Basingstoke: Palgrave Macmillan.

Parker, J. E. K. (2015). *Acoustic Jurisprudence*. New York: Oxford University Press.

Party, D. (2009). Placer Culpable: Shame and Nostalgia in the 1990s Chilean *Balada* Revival. *Revista de Música Latonamericana*, **30**(1), 69–98, 114.

Pedwell, C. (2014). *Affective Relations: The Transnational Politics of Empathy*. Basingstoke: Palgrave Macmillan.

Pettan, S., and Titon, J. T., eds. (2015). *The Oxford Handbook of Applied Ethnomusicology*. New York: Oxford University Press.

Phillips-Hutton, A., and Nielsen, N. (In press). Ethics. In T. McAuley, N. Nielsen, J. Levinson, and A. Phillips-Hutton, eds., *The Oxford Handbook of Western Music and Philosophy*. New York: Oxford University Press, pp. 283–306.

Pilger, J. (2014). Another Stolen Generation. *The Guardian*. 21 March. https://bit.ly/328C3MS (accessed 7 January 2020).

Pilzer, J. D. (2012). *Hearts of Pine: Songs in the Lives of Three Korean Survivors of the Japanese 'Comfort Women'*. New York: Oxford University Press.

Pilzer, J. D. (2014). Music and Dance in the Japanese Military 'Comfort Women' System: A Case Study in the Performing Arts, War, and Sexual Violence. *Women and Music: A Journal of Gender and Culture*, **18**(1), 1–23.

Pinto García, M. E. (2014). Music and Reconciliation in Colombia: Opportunities and Limitations of Songs Composed by Victims. *Music and Arts in Action*, **4**(2), 24–51.

Pruitt, L. (2011). Music, Youth, and Peacebuilding in Northern Ireland. *Global Change, Peace and Security*, **23**(2), 207–22.

Putnam, D. A. (1987). Why Instrumental Music Has No Shame. *The British Journal of Aesthetics*, **27**(1), 55–61.

Rabinowich, T.-C., Cross, I., and Burnard, P. (2013). Long-term Musical Group Interaction has a Positive Influence on Empathy in Children. *Psychology of Music*, **41**(4), 484–98.

Ramsbotham, O., Woodhouse, T., and Miall, H. (2011). *Contemporary Conflict Resolution*, 3rd ed. Cambridge: Polity Press.

Rayner, B. (2016). Not a Soul left Untouched at Roy Thomson Hall by Gord Downie's Secret Path. *The Star*. 21 October. https://bit.ly/3kYegb8 (accessed 7 January 2020).

Read, P. (2006). The Stolen Generations: The Removal of Aboriginal Children in New South Wales 1883–1969. 4th ed. New South Wales Department of Aboriginal Affairs. https://bit.ly/3aHBU7k (accessed 7 January 2020).

Rice, T. (2017). Ethnomusicology in Times of Trouble. In *Modeling Ethnomusicology*. New York: Oxford University Press, pp. 233–54.

Rickwood, J. (2013). We are Australian: An Ethnographic Investigation of the Convergence of Community Music and Reconciliation. PhD thesis, Australian National University.

Rieff, D. (2016). *In Praise of Forgetting*. New Haven, CT: Yale University Press.

Ritter, J. (2014). The 'Voice of the Victims': Testimonial Songs in Rural Ayacucho. In C. E. Milton, ed., *Art from a Fractured Past: Memory and Truth-Telling in Post-Shining Path Peru*. Durham, NC: Duke University Press, pp. 217–53.

Robertson, C. (2008). Music and Conflict Transformation in Bosnia: Constructing and Reconstructing the Normal. *Music and the Arts in Action*, **2**(2), 38–55.

Rosen, J. W. (2014). Dissident 'Choirboy': Rwandan Gospel Star on Trial. *Al-Jazeera America*. 11 December. https://bit.ly/2Emebx5 (accessed 20 August 2020).

Rothberg, M. (2019). *The Implicated Subject: Beyond Victims and Perpetrators*. Stanford, CA: Stanford University Press.

Saarikallio, S. (2010). Music as Emotional Self-Regulation throughout Adulthood. *Psychology of Music*, **39**(3), 307–27.

Sandole, D. J. (1998). A Comprehensive Mapping of Conflict and Conflict Resolution Research: A Three Pillar Approach. *Peace and Conflict Studies*, **5**(2), 1–30.

Scruton, R. (2014). Music and Morality. *Disputatio: Philosophical Research Bulletin*, **4**, 33–48.

Sedgwick, E. K. (2003). *Touching Feeling: Affect, Pedagogy, Performativity*. Durham, NC: Duke University Press.

Seeds of Peace. (2006). Sharon Stone Supports Seeds of Peace. 31 October. www.seedsofpeace.org/sharon-stone-supports-seeds-of-peace/ (accessed 7 January 2020).

Skyllstad, K. (1995). Society in Harmony: A Polyaesthetic School-Program for Interracial Understanding. *History of European Ideas*, **20**(1), 89–97.

Skyllstad, K. (2000). Creating a Culture of Peace: The Performing Arts in Interethnic Negotiations. *Intercultural Communication*, 4, n.p. https://immi.se/intercultural/nr4/skyllstad.htm

Skyllstad, K. (2008). Managing Conflicts through Music: Educational Perspectives. In O. Urbain, ed., *Music and Conflict Transformation: Harmonies and Dissonances in Geopolitics*. London: I.B. Tauris & Co., pp. 172–86.

Small, C. (1998). *Musicking: The Meanings of Performance and Listening*. Middletown, CT: Wesleyan University Press.

Softic, B. (2011). The Music of Srebrenica after the War. *Nar. Umjet*, **48**(1), 161–81.

Sprigge, M. (2019). Dresden's Musical Ruins. *Journal of the Royal Musical Association*, **144**(1), 83–121.

Stein, E. (1989) *On the Problem of Empathy*. Translated by Waltraut Stein. 3rd ed. Washington, DC: ICS Publications.

Stige, B., Ansdell, G., Elefant, C., and Pavlicevic, M. (2010). *Where Music Helps: Community Music Therapy in Action and Reflection*. Aldershot: Ashgate.

Stirling, C. (2018). Sound, Affect, Politics. In M. Bull, ed., *The Routledge Companion to Sound Studies*. New York: Routledge, pp. 54–67.

Stokes, M. (2006). Adam Smith and the Dark Nightingale: On Twentieth-Century Sentimentalism. *Twentieth-Century Music*, **3**(2), 201–19.

Stokes, M. (2010). *Republic of Love: Cultural Intimacy in Turkish Popular Music*. Chicago, IL: The University of Chicago Press.

Sugarman, J. (2010). Kosova Calls for Peace: Song, Myth and War in an Age of Global Media. In J. M. O'Connell and S. Castelo-Branco, eds., *Music and Conflict*. Champaign, IL: University of Illinois Press, pp. 17–45.

Taylor, D. (2003). *The Archive and the Repertoire: Performing Cultural Memory in the Americas*. Durham, NC: Duke University Press.

The Observer. (2006). Barenboim's Harmonious Message Goes Beyond Classical Music. 30 April. https://bit.ly/2FEDKdF (accessed 7 January 2020).

Thompson, E. (2001). Empathy and Consciousness. *Journal of Consciousness Studies*, **8**(5–7), 1–32.

Tobin, M. (2007). School Bans 'Sorry Song'. *The World Today*, Australian Broadcasting Corporation. 11 July. www.abc.net.au/worldtoday/content/2007/s1975739.htm (accessed 7 January 2020).

Tomkins, S. (1995). *Shame and its Sisters: A Silvan Tomkins Reader*. E. K. Sedgewick and A. Frank, eds. Durham, NC: Duke University Press.

TRC of Canada. (2015a). *Canada's Residential Schools: The History, Part 2, 1939 to 2000, vol. 1*. Montreal: McGill-Queen's University Press.

TRC of Canada. (2015b). Honouring the Truth, Reconciling for the Future: Summary of the Final Report of the Truth and Reconciliation Commission of Canada. https://bit.ly/2YiqTnY (accessed 20 August 2020).

Turino, T. (2008). *Music as Social Life: The Politics of Participation*. Chicago, IL: University of Chicago Press.

Turner, V. (1969). *The Ritual Process*. Chicago, IL: Aldine.

United Nations. (2010). United Nations Approach to Transitional Justice, Guidance Notes of the Secretary-General. https://bit.ly/3hoJYMR (accessed 7 January 2020).

United Nations. (2016). West–Eastern Divan Orchestra Designated United Nations Global Advocate for Cultural Understanding. www.un.org/press/en/2016/pi2154.doc.htm (accessed 1 July 2020).

Urbain, O. (2008). Introduction. In O. Urbain, ed., *Music and Conflict Transformation: Harmonies and Dissonances in Geopolitics*. London: I.B. Tauris & Co., pp. 1–9.

Villa-Vicencio, C. (1999). Living in the Wake of the Truth and Reconciliation Commission: A Retroactive Reflection. *Law, Democracy and Development*, **3**(2), 195–208.

Warren, J. (2014). *Music and Ethical Responsibility*. Cambridge: Cambridge University Press.

Watt, D. (2007). Toward a Neuroscience of Empathy: Integrating Affective and Cognitive Perspectives. *Neuropsychoanalysis*, **9**(2), 119–40.

Weschler, L. (1989). Afterword. In L. Weschler, ed., *State Crimes: Punishment or Pardon*. Queenstown, MD: Justice and Society Program of the Aspen Institute, pp. 89–93.

Wheeler, B. (2016). Gord Downie's *Secret Path* Delivers on Its Heavy Ambition. *The Globe and Mail*. 18 October.

Williams, B. (1993). *Shame and Necessity*. Berkeley, CA: University of California Press.

Williams, B. (2006). *Ethics and the Limits of Philosophy*. London: Routledge.

Young, M. (2014). Australia in the Grip of a New 'Stolen Generation'. *News*. 2 August. https://bit.ly/3gjjLOp (accessed 7 January 2020).

Zelizer, C. (2003). The Role of Artistic Processes in Peace-Building in Bosnia-Herzegovina. *Peace and Conflict Studies*, **10**(2), 62–75.

Acknowledgements

I am particularly grateful to Kerry Fletcher, Jo Randell, Mike Downie, and Stuart Coxe for their generosity in sharing audiovisual materials with me. In addition, special thanks are due to Nicholas Cook, Alexander Phillips-Hutton, B. Darwin, and Mr Edward Bear for their invaluable feedback.

Cambridge Elements ⁼

Music since 1945

Mervyn Cooke
University of Nottingham

Mervyn Cooke brings to the role of series editor an unusually broad range of expertise, having published widely in the fields of twentieth-century opera, concert and theatre music, jazz, and film music. He has edited and co-edited *Cambridge Companions to Britten, Jazz, Twentieth-Century Opera*, and *Film Music*. His other books include *Britten: War Requiem, Britten and the Far East, A History of Film Music, The Hollywood Film Music Reader, Pat Metheny: The ECM Years*, and two illustrated histories of jazz. He is currently co-editing (with Christopher R. Wilson) *The Oxford Handbook of Shakespeare and Music*.

About the Series

Elements in Music since 1945 is a highly stimulating collection of authoritative online essays that reflects the latest research into a wide range of musical topics of international significance since the Second World War. Individual Elements are organised into constantly evolving clusters devoted to such topics as art music, jazz, music and image, stage and screen genres, music and media, music and place, immersive music, music and movement, music and politics, music and conflict, and music and society. The latest research questions in theory, criticism, musicology, composition, and performance are also given cutting-edge and thought-provoking coverage. The digital-first format allows authors to respond rapidly to new research trends, with contributions being updated to reflect the latest thinking in their fields, and the essays are enhanced by the provision of an exciting range of online resources.

Cambridge Elements ≡

Music since 1945

Elements in the Series

Music Transforming Conflict
Ariana Phillips-Hutton

Herbert Eimert and the Darmstadt School: The Consolidation of the Avant-Garde
Max Erwin

A full series listing is available at: www.cambridge.org/core/what-we-publish/
elements/music-since-1945

Printed in the United States
By Bookmasters